D1757641

# ON CRAFTSMANSHIP

Christopher Frayling

# On Craftsmanship

*towards a new Bauhaus*

OBERON BOOKS

LONDON

First published in 2011 by Oberon Books Ltd

521 Caledonian Road, London N7 9RH

Tel: 020 7607 3637 / Fax: 020 7607 3629

e-mail: info@oberonbooks.com

www.oberonbooks.com

Reprinted in 2012, 2014

A catalogue record for this book is available from the British Library.

ISBN: 978-1-84943-072-2

Printed and bound by Replika Press Pvt Ltd, India

# *Contents*

# *Introduction*

CRAFTSMANSHIP HAS AGAIN become fashionable in high places, just as it did during the last few recessions. In the boom times of the early 2000s, the public talk was of design: now it is more of craft, a shift which mirrors the parallel move from 'the creative industries' to 'productive industry' and manufacturing. Government ministers extol 'the joy of technical accomplishment, the beauty of craft skills [in schools]' and stress the need for a new, updated Arts and Crafts movement to re-energise good old British inventiveness. There is talk of bringing back long-forgotten technical schools. Policy buffs discuss the 'parity of esteem' between intellectual and practical pursuits, ways of reviving guilds and apprenticeships, whether 'making' properly belongs in higher or further education or both. Too many crafts, one minister has argued, 'have been given an academic veneer ... [which has] done academic study no favours': better to think of the crafts as *vocational*. Others prefer to celebrate the achievements of the crafts and design within universities. In the United States, Professor Matthew Crawford – a philosopher who also runs a motorcycle repair shop specialising in old European and Japanese models – has published an impassioned and best-selling *Case For Working With Your Hands or Why Office Work is Bad for Us and Fixing Things Feels Good* (originally entitled *Shop*

*Class as Soul Craft – an enquiry into the value of work* (2009)), which argues the morality of getting one's hands dirty by actually making and fixing things, an argument which tries hard to 'avoid the precious images of manual work that intellectuals sometimes traffic in'. *The Case* relates to the current economic climate in a similar way to Robert Pirsig's *Zen and the Art of Motorcycle Maintenance* in the mid-1970s – with less Plato and more Aristotle – and it has made a surprising splash with political analysts on this side of the Atlantic. Are people less likely to throw things away these days? Has the knowledge economy rhetoric been overdone? What about the things you can't get on the internet – like hammering a nail or driving a screw – the things that have to be performed in person, the things that can't be flown over from China or supplied down the wire.

Meanwhile, Alain de Botton has assembled *The Pleasures and Sorrows of Work* (2009), a collage of examples around the question 'when does a job feel meaningful'. And New York sociologist Richard Sennett has, in *The Craftsman* (2008), examined 'the desire to do a job well for its own sake' – from historical, sociological and philosophical perspectives – as *the* characteristic that distinguishes us from other life forms. He is convinced the desire resides in all of us.

So craftsmanship is definitely in the ether, as an idea ripe to be 'reclaimed', 're-evaluated' and 'redefined' – an idea that should shed its tendency to speak its name with a cringe, an upward cadence of the voice. Let's hear it for making things as best we can.

But ... 'craftsmanship' and 'the crafts' are not as simple as they sound.

The commonsense definition of the word 'craft' seems clear enough: an activity which involves skill in making things by hand; derived from the old English *craeft* – meaning strength or skill. But on closer inspection the word becomes more and more difficult to pin down – a short word that has been stretched in recent years almost to breaking point. Big manufacturers like to promote their wares with the language of craft – 'hand-made', 'hand-finished', 'made by our craftsmen', 'uniquely for you' – cousin of the language of 'organic', to reassure their anxious customers. Recent global campaigns using the imagery of craft have included Levi's 'Craftwork' – with sixteen London craftworkers as 'the face of the campaign' – and Camper's 'Extraordinary Crafts' range of shoes, revealing through a piece of performance art that 'creativity has been applied to every process'. The word 'craft' is usually assumed by the ad-people to be associated in the public mind with the values of the recent past rather than the present, with the good old pre-digital days. And some products still, apparently, embody these values. The assumption is that when you are in danger of losing something, it becomes specially precious to you. This, at the same time as manuals of business management and public administration have been hijacking the language of the Modernist avant-garde (usually the Bauhaus) to show how forward-thinking they have become – 'fitness for purpose', 'making the form follow the function', 'out of the box', not to mention any number of palettes, sculptings, broad-brushes, frames of reference, patinas, cutting-edges, templates, tools, tool-boxes, stonewallings, carvings of niches, building of brands and cuttings of one's coat according to one's cloth.

It all depends on where you are coming from. To a sociologist, the word 'craft' is associated with 'skilled manual labour' or 'the aristocracy of labour'. To an economist, with a stage in economic development preceding capitalism (there are overlaps and fusions between the two stages). To an anthropologist, with the maker as user, with *homo faber* or the maker of things and *homo ludens* or the 'deep play' of everyday life. To a countryman, with traditional rural pursuits. To a literary historian, with the anti-establishment stance of the Romantics. To a trade unionist, with a community of skilled people defending the way they perform their occupations. To a laboratory scientist, with the use of equipment to *do science* – a contemporary version of Galileo's dialogue between Galileo the astronomer and Galileo the builder of the telescope, the 'starry messenger'. In Germany during the 1920s-1930s, the culture of 'craft' – and of anti-modernism – was strongly associated with the political Right; in Britain during the 1880s-1890s – through the writings of William Morris, Walter Crane and disciples – with the political Left: similar repertoire of arguments, radically opposed conclusions. In Germany, this became a popular movement, centred on disaffected artisanal businesses; in Britain, it was mainly confined to the artistic realm and was much better tempered. All in the name of craft. Policy-makers today prefer to see 'craft' as a stimulus to local or regional economies, skills and materials, sometimes in relation to wider networks. To an art critic, the word 'craft' is about the distinction between an 'art' – as in intellectual/conceptual – and a 'mere craft' – as in manual – a debased version of age-old debates about the social recognition of the artist which go back to the Italian Renaissance, sharpened in England by Royal patronage of 'fine artists'. On this one, Turner prize-winner Grayson Perry recently delivered a show-stopper: 'I think the art world had more trouble coming to terms with me being a potter than with my choice of frocks.... If you call your pot 'art' you are being pretentious; but if you call your shark 'art' you are being philosophical!' So – ironically – to an art school-educated craftsperson, the word now has unfortunate associations with manual skill which rather get in the way of making art. To a designer, 'craft' is about the workmanship of risk and – most recently – the slow design movement. Meanwhile, artist Damien Hirst has confessed that the word 'skill' always reminds him of macramé

To educationalists, on the other hand, the word is associated with learning by doing – experiential learning – rather than learning from books or from screens, the 'c' word which since the 1990s has been dropped from the title of English secondary school design curricula, when 'craft, design and technology' morphed into 'design and technology', but which may be on its way back again: a recent survey of why 'design and technology' courses were proving so popular in some schools with GCSE pupils, especially boys, concluded that up to 75% of them wanted to go on and design computer games. The crafts were first introduced into the school curriculum in the early 1880s, 'to teach the hand and eye in unison' and 'to familiarise pupils with the properties of materials'. The idea was that this might help remove the social stigma attached in British society to manual occupations. The phrase 'parity of esteem' was much used, then as now. It didn't work. Today, with the decline of laboratory work in school science, and the transformation of design into a briefing process, 'making' is at its lowest ebb since before the Arts and Crafts Movement. Can it come back?

To a viewer of mid-evening television, the word 'craft' is to do with watching from a distance as acknowledged experts show what they can do with cookery, gardening, singing, fishing, survivalism, nature-watching, interior designing, doing up a house – while sometimes encouraging less skilled punters to have a go for themselves. Or with television documentaries about extreme occupations – trawlermen, firefighters, steeplejacks – which are the polar opposite of *The Office* where many of the viewers must actually work.

If you look up the word 'craft' in Brewer's, it offers 'name given to freemasonry by its members', in other words a mysterious form of knowledge, a black box, a usage which seems to date from 1014 BC and the building of Solomon's Temple: in the words of the Authorised Version of the Old Testament, 'and they brought great stones, costly stones, and hewed stones, to lay the foundation of the house. And [the] builders did hew them, and the stone-squarers: so they prepared timber and stones to build the house'. The word can be a verb or a noun – but the adjective 'crafty' and the adverb 'craftily', as in deceitful, mean almost the opposite of the usual definitions of craft. Shakespeare played on this when he had King Richard II talk of 'wooing poor crafts-men with the craft of smiles'. If, on the other hand, you were to enquire in a residential care home what the initials C-R-A-F-T stand for, the reply would more than likely be 'can't remember a f.....g thing'.

And if someone were to approach you and ask 'what do you make?' and you were to reply 'oh, I make *things* and I make them as well as I can', chances are the questioner would be at a loss for words. Because the question 'what do you make?' is really about how much you earn or how big your bonus is, not '*what* do you make?' at all. At the same time, the word 'product' has moved on from meaning 'a thing assembled or manufac-tured' to meaning a bundle of services – a word to be attached to anything produced by any business. Similarly, the word 'Design' with a big 'D' has given birth to a small 'd' offshoot which in the jargon is about design management/organisation/strategy; about conceptualising and planning in general. Not about things any more, or not only about things, because we are increasingly living on thin air. So looser words such as 'creativity' and 'innovation' often seem a more comfortable fit.

And yet, as Richard Sennett's *The Craftsman* has forcefully argued, the concept of 'craft' – meaning at its broadest 'a basic human impulse, the desire to do a job well for its own sake' (let's leave 'skill' to one side for the moment) – has in some ways never been as relevant and timely as it is today.

Craftsmanship is assailed on all sides by – among other tendencies – flexible working, portfolio careers, multi-tasking, short-terminism, quick-fix training, suspicion of expertise, confusion between elites and elitism, the downgrading of dedication, quantitative targets and tick-boxing, the value attached to presentation skills and the rise of semiotic man, out-sourcing offshore, 'we'll write it they'll print it', casino capitalism, the 'look at me!' culture, fifteen minutes of fame, branding, one size fits all, the remote society, the rapidity of technological change and, as Sennett puts it, the omnipresence of 'sharks and incompetents' of all descriptions 'who have no trouble succeeding'. Quite a list! Against these – and more – he argues that craft, the pleasure in making and the time taken in improving skills are just as important to the functioning of a modern society as they were in the medieval era of the Guilds. Not in a romantic sense, though. Sennett tries hard to demythologise the concept of craftsmanship, rooting it in material reality and material consciousness, preferring to find nourishment in Diderot and

D'Alembert's eighteenth-century *Encyclopédie* – where artisanal occupations and mental labour are treated as on a par with each other, where doing a job well involves as well as physical activity submerged processes of reflection and feeling, where the crafts are a form of social capital handed down from master to apprentice – than in nineteenth-century laments for the world we have lost. The crafts in his very broad definition are not primarily about looking backwards. But they do involve hard work and dedication: it takes 10,000 hours of practice to become a skilled carpenter or musician – that's three hours a day for ten years. Sennett goes well beyond the world of the traditional craftsman, such as (his favourite examples) the cathedral-builders, Benvenuto Cellini, Antonio Stradivari and Christopher Wren, to modern-day examples of craftsmanship as varied as nursing, mothering, Japanese car assembly, open source software and linked digital workshops where he sees the real possibility of a community of craftspeople who embody some of the elements celebrated by Homer in the ancient story of the lame god Hephaestus 'sweating in toil and busy about his bellows'. Some see the information society as antithetical to physical acts of making. Sennett doesn't. Others have written of the craftsmanship involved in the processes and products of nanotechnology, or in using digital sensors and actuators.

Whether or not Sennett's example of customising open source software is entirely convincing, the questions asked in

*The Craftsman* are certainly timely and may even be urgent. As I say, craftsmanship is definitely in the ether again.

My interest in the subject has many roots. My great-grandfather Daniel Imhof made 'Orchestrions' – or mechanical musical instruments – in a water-powered workshop in South Germany, and sold them through his shop in New Oxford Street, London. So maybe some of Daniel is in my DNA. I went to a junior school which specialised in the arts and crafts, run by the sister of the Arctic explorer Wilfred Hampton, and a primary school where the woodwork shop, the ceramics studio and the weaving room were central to the curriculum. The sense of achievement in completing a table-mat, a pot or a piece of multicoloured woven fabric – the sense of understanding things, experiencing them, learning how to do them and getting tangible results – is still with me after all these years. Of how many other classroom subjects can that be said? The school was just down the road from Ditchling, with its strong arts and crafts connections dating back to the post-William Morris era. As an undergraduate, I first encountered Jean-Jacques Rousseau's treatise on education *Emile* (1762) with its deeply felt arguments against learning by rote and social conditioning in favour of the development of the individual child – what would today more prosaically be called, after Piaget, the 'psycho-genetic' educational principle. Book III of *Emile*, dealing with the early teenage years, is concerned with the learning of a craft (in his case carpentry): 'If, instead of making a child stick to his books, I employ him in a workshop, his hands work to the advantage of his intellect, he becomes a philosopher while he thinks he is simply becoming an artisan ...' This made a profound impression on me and I often revisited *Emile*. Immanuel Kant called the publication of the book an event comparable in significance to the French Revolution – which is pushing it, though *Emile* was certainly revolutionary in its implications in its time and even now.

Then, during my thirty-six years of working at the Royal College of Art, from part-time tutor to Rector – in a tight-knit community of talented postgraduate artists, designers and craftspeople – I frequently discussed, debated and tried to encourage high standards of craftsmanship in practice and in thinking. At the end of the 1970s, I supervised a thesis on 'Craftsmanship in the Machine Environment' by Helen Snowdon (who would later become my wife) and this, too, proved a life-changing experience in many different ways. It often occurred to me at that time, and still does, that compared with art and design, the crafts have a lot of catching-up to do. And, from the word go, I always resented the prejudice of some of my more academic colleagues from the ancient universities, that craftsmanship is 'merely vocational', something to be done with the hands *rather than* with the head. I vividly remember my first meeting of the Committee of the Vice-Chancellors (as it was then called), when I asked why *performance* was not more highly valued in music departments, and the head of one of these ancient universities responded by asking which institution I was representing.

'The Royal College of Art', I replied. 'Oh, isn't that where they mend fuses?' At the time, I couldn't think of a suitable reply. What I should have said – the spirit of the staircase later came to me – was that a thorough education in the practice of the crafts (performing, musical and visual) actually predates the rise of even the ancient universities. And that they definitely belong in higher education, alongside the academics who interpret the world.

The essays in this book, written over that thirty-six-year period, have in their different ways tried to address many of the issues surrounding 'the crafts' and 'craftsmanship' which have recently resurfaced. There was the need to see through misty-eyed accounts of the historical crafts, in order to have a sensible debate about them in the present day. The need to rid the concept of its Gilbertian tendency to 'pooh-pooh whatever's fresh and new'. There was the continuing influence of 'making' in any fully-rounded education: less a question of reading, writing, rithmetic (which are actually two Rs, literacy and numeracy) than a question of reading, *wroughting*, rithmetic (the real three Rs), even at a time when technical skills are being increasingly undervalued in the wider society. Then there were the hotly contested meanings of the word 'skill' – are they lost or are they redistributed?; some classic literary accounts of craftsmanship and their legacies; the distinction between formal knowledge and tacit knowledge (which I introduced into the debate about the crafts, from its philosophical origins); the shifting boundaries and hierarchies between art and craft on the one hand and craft and design on the other – which are partly about fashion and style rather than substance and are in any case specific to the culture of the West; the issue of whether or not 'the new technology' has driven a definitive wedge between the creation of objects and the skills of the craftsman; and, nearly a hundred years after the original Bauhaus, what a 'new Bauhaus' in the changed contexts of the twenty-first century might be like. The occasionally embattled tone of these essays has to do with the purposes for which they were originally written: to counter a crafts revivalism of an over-sentimental kind – the tweed and Viyella check shirt variety; to establish the place of the crafts and design in the curricula of schools and universities, bringing together the head and the hand; to explore the rise of conceptual art and its implications for the skills of making *and* for collectors who want to buy tangible *things;* to contribute to then-passionate debates about the contemporary meanings of craftsmanship; to relate these to gender; and to reflect on the long process of absorbing the lessons of digital technologies.

In the end, much of what I have written about craftsmanship over the years has been – and is – concerned with the issue to which the playwright Tom Stoppard has often returned in his very elegant conversations on the stage about modern art, for example in *Artist Descending a Staircase* (1972):

> Skill without imagination is craftsmanship and gives
> us many useful objects such as wickerwork picnic
> baskets. Imagination without skill gives us modern art!

I don't agree. And these pieces in their different ways try to explain why.

# Acknowledgements

These essays, which began life as articles, reviews and lectures and which have been revised or tweaked for new publication, first appeared in: *Craft History One* (October 1988), *The Schoolmaster and the Wheelwrights*; *Designer* (May 1984), *Forever Ambridge*; *Issues in Design Education*, edited by the late David Thistlewood (Longman 1990) and *Crafts* magazine (January 1982), *Skill – a word to start an argument*; *Beyond the Dovetail – craft, skill and imagination*, edited Christopher Frayling (Crafts Council, 1991), *The Professor of Digging* and *Things Men Have Made*; *2D/3D – art and craft made and designed in the 20ᵗʰ Century* (Northern Centre for Contemporary Art, 1987), *The Medium and the Message*; *Crafts* (March 2003), *Shape Shifting*; and *Art Libraries Journal* (vol 32, 1, 2007), *The New Bauhaus*. I would like to thank the three graces of contemporary craft – Marigold Coleman (now Wace), Barley Roscoe and Martina Margetts – for their advice and help; Danny Weil, Ron Arad, Martin Smith, Liz Aylieff, David Hamilton, David Watkins, Michael

Rowe, Clare Johnston, Mary Restieaux, Joanne Brogden and Wendy Dagworthy – and all the students in their respective departments at the Royal College of Art – for directly or indirectly shaping the ideas in this book. Also the late – and much missed – Peter Dormer. Above all my wife Helen, to whom it is lovingly dedicated. The book wouldn't have happened without her and it wouldn't have been nearly so enjoyable either.

# 1. The Schoolmaster and the Wheelwrights

G EORGE STURT'S BOOK *The Wheelwright's Shop* was written between 1920 and 1921. It describes events which had occurred at 84 East Street, Farnham some 30 years before. For many readers and craft practitioners it is a classic account – perhaps even *the* classic account – of a particular craft written 'from the inside': not a soft-focus evocation of a craft, written by someone who occasionally does a spot of gardening and who consequently thinks that manual labour is terrific fun; nor a coffee-table book, using all the latest technology to tell us that most of the latest technology is all bad; but an unpretentious little book which – for all sorts of reasons – has steadily acquired an enormous critical reputation. Partly, the current reputation of *The Wheelwright's Shop* is due to the fact that – like so many of the nostalgic reminiscences written or compiled during the British agricultural depression of the 1920s – it seems to strike a distinct chord today, a time when retrospective regret has become both fashionable and commercially exploitable; at a time when 'villages of the mind' are an established part of haute culture. Partly, the reputation dates from the 1930s, when cultural analysts such as F.R. Leavis and Denys Thompson turned *The Wheelwright's Shop* into a key text from the great tradition of English literature, an embodiment of age-old values which were thought at the time to be seriously under threat from the twin forces of 'Americanism' and 'modern economic life'.

But the importance of George Sturt's *The Wheelwright's Shop* seems to me to go well beyond the contemporary nostalgia boom and the inter-war fascination with the world we have lost – although both of these have ensured the book a very wide circulation. *The Wheelwright's Shop* remains a major contribution to the understanding of that much-misunderstood term 'craftsmanship', which can be read, even today, at many different levels. The theme which holds the work together is the theme of a schoolmaster trying hard – sometimes embarrassingly hard – to understand exactly what a small group of craftspeople actually *do*. As such, the book is of considerable interest to anyone who seeks to write about the practice of a particular craft, from an historical *or* a contemporary point of view. And since Sturt's earliest published writings, in the mid to late 1880s, were congruent with the social theories of William Morris, the way in which he originally approached the subject is of considerable interest as well.

At one level, *The Wheelwright's Shop* is the chronicle of a transformation within one particular productive activity – from handicraft to a small assembly line; from the Surrey wagon to the traction engine; from William Morris, Victorian socialist, to William Morris, automobile magnate – with due emphasis given to each of the stages in this transformation: the abandonment of 'Saint Monday' and the traditional holidays; regular hours of work; clocking in; the arrival of systematic management in the form of a manager named William Goatcher, appointed from outside; the attempt to speed up the production process in order to attract local farmers; and, finally, the introduction of new technology and the change from craft workshop to garage. At another level, as the cultural analysts of the 1930s were quick to point out, it *appears* to be a sustained lament for the 'passing of Old England' – a lament which uses words like 'craftsmanship', 'handwork' and 'skill' in a fairly sentimental way, to heighten the contrast: the most interesting thing about *this* theme is that Sturt occasionally stood outside it, showing himself to be very aware of what he was thinking 'naturally'. In his *Journal* of 1899, he wrote that it was very dangerous to romanticise the past, to indulge in Merrie Englandism, or to expect to gatecrash the 'comely social life' described in Goldsmith's *Deserted Village*; at one point, he even suggested that a sure way to prevent present nostalgia was to imagine the nostalgia with which future genera-tions (from 'anno 2000, say') would describe the 1890s, for their own purposes. A woman wrote to him, shortly after the publica-tion of his most popular book at the time, *Change in the Village*, complaining that 'the old village life was not so nice in reality as I have made out,' to which Sturt could only reply that conversa-tions with some local villagers went 'far to bear out the truth of what she urges', and that life was 'squalid or at any rate rough and insanitary'. 'I *would not go back,'* he later wrote, 'I would not lift a finger, or say a word, to restore the past time' – for to do so would be to 'harden into a hide-bound conservative', the worst kind of antiquarian. Nevertheless, he chose to ignore much of the squalor, and the vague feeling that his employees the wheelwrights might have resented his presence all along, when he constructed his picture of *The Wheelwright's Shop* in the early 1920s.

At yet another level, the book is a detailed illustrated account of the techniques of the wheelwrights as Sturt eventually came to understand them – for the record, so that they would not be lost forever – and in particular of the ways in which these techniques had slowly adapted (or not) to changing material circumstances: the section of the book devoted to the 'dish' shape of a cartwheel is the most famous example, but there are many others such as Sturt's description of the 'putting on' of metal tyres.

And finally, we come to what is from my point of view the most important level, the attempts by Sturt the schoolmaster to enter the 'invisible college' represented by the wheelwrights, an invisible college which represented for him a radical change of social and intellectual direction. The phrase 'invisible college', by the way, originated during the Commonwealth period, when it was applied to what was later to become the Royal Society. In sociological analysis, it has come to mean a social circle which is distinguished by the greater density of relations between its members than between members and non-members. Some sociologists have seen 'invisible colleges' as the social location of distinctive sets of 'technical and cognitive norms'; others have simply seen them as the social location for a particular set of shared assumptions.

George Sturt took over the management and trading of the family wheelwright's shop in 1884, at the age of 21. His father, Francis Sturt, who had been 'made a wheelwright' from an early age, had managed the shop since 1865, when *he* had inherited it from George Sturt senior. In the book *The Wheelwright's Shop*, which was put together some thirty years ago after the event, Sturt has very little to say about the circumstances of the changeover:

> In 1884 he died; and I, for my part, did not know how to carry on even the ordinary business. I had no more than a month, if as much as that, of my father's guidance in it. He was, in fact, sickening for his last illness, when I entered the business in 1884. Ruskin's *Fors Clavigera* had made me think meanly, if not meanly enough, of the school teaching which had been my work since 1878; and under the same influence of Ruskin's book I felt that man's only decent occupation was in handicraft. I shudder yet smile to think now what raw ideas swayed me then; yet the enthusiasm so ill-reflected in them was the sweetness of life to me in every disillusionment that was to come. They saved me from the worst sordidness of business. Finishing

> my school work with the first term of 1884, namely the
> day before Good Friday, I took four days of rest …and
> began work at the shop on Easter Tuesday.

The picture is of an idealistic young schoolmaster who has gleaned all sorts of images of the arts and crafts from his reading of Ruskin – in particular the idea that 'man's only decent occupation was in handicraft' – and who is providentially chosen by his father, at just the right moment, to continue the family tradition. Actually, as Sturt's personal *Journal* shows (and there are over 4000 manuscript pages of it, kept in the British Library), this was far from the case. In the first place, his brother Frank was originally the man chosen to take over the business: he was the son who *knew* something about the trade ('he had more practice in some parts of it than I ever enjoyed'), but the wheelwrights gave him such a rough time ('insulting him with covert innuendo') – and he appears to have responded to this so clumsily – that he 'faded out' after two years, in the early 1880s. In the second place, Sturt's departure from Farnham Grammar School was not entirely on account of what he was later to call his 'Ruskinian absurdities'. Ever since 1879 he had been teaching Geometry and Drawing as a pupil teacher, and since 1873 he had been a regular attender at the drawing classes held at Farnham Art School, then in the Town Hall. But throughout the early 1880s he was plagued by the asthma he had contracted before he was twelve months old and by a series of attacks of bronchitis. Long hours in the classroom did not suit either his temperament or his health and there is evidence that he rapidly became disillusioned with a world of 'children that vex and colleagues that are distasteful'. He was, he later said, in danger of 'knowing everything and being trained to do next to nothing', and he was convinced that most of the teaching was in the interests of the educators rather than of the pupils. His commitment to the task seems to have steadily diminished as he felt more and more like a painter painting a picture of someone painting a picture of someone painting a picture, in other words as he lost all personal engagement with the subjects he was supposed to be teaching. Add to this his firm conviction that he would in time have been moulded into a 'commodity in the teaching market', and you have more than sufficient reason for his honourable discharge from the Grammar School – without recourse to the works of John Ruskin.

But the Ruskin reference does provide one clue to the kinds of problem encountered by the schoolmaster as he attempted to adjust to life in the shop. For Sturt left the school with ambitions to contribute to the public debate about art and society, with which both Ruskin and William Morris were associated in his mind, and in the early years at 84 East Street he spent every hour of his leisure – the hour between six and seven in the morning, and the hours after eight at night – on 'literary exercises, anything that seemed to uplift me above the sordid cares (as I thought them) that would come with daylight'. In retrospect Sturt concluded that his mind was 'priggishly puffed up' for most of this time, but the *Journal* of 1890 is full of sentiments like 'If I had some *regular* work – literature – that I could always turn to, would not much of my best time be saved? At least I should have less temptation to spend my activity on ledgers or bills and these are surely well enough served in moments more dull….'

Throughout this early period at the shop, Sturt sustained a lively correspondence with the novelist Arnold Bennett, who acted as his informal literary agent and who insisted on addressing him from London as 'my dear villager'. Bennett was convinced that 'Writing occupies *all* his thoughts in a way I had never suspected. With the most perfect naturalness, he regards everything as "material"…. A more literary temperament than his it would be difficult to conceive.'

Bennett was equally convinced that Sturt's many complaints about the amount of time he had to spend in the shop were simply excuses to put off the inevitable day when he would decide to write full-time: 'I know that your "foreman", or some other legendary griffin with claws worries you, but I fail to rid myself of the idea that what you want is simple steam….' The thing that Arnold Bennett did not understand (for the simple reason that Sturt never told him) was that George Sturt *had* to keep up the family business – two unmarried sisters, Susan and Mary, were entirely dependent on the wheelwright's shop for their income.

Nevertheless, the *Journal* reveals that Sturt thought seriously about selling the shop twice before his thirtieth birthday; the first time in January 1891 when he wrote that the petty affairs at East Street were sapping his will to live; and again in 1894 when he applied (probably unsuccessfully) for a civil service post in the Department of Science and Art. In 1891 a solution was found in the person of William Goatcher, coach-builder, who was engaged as 'foreman-manager' to take some of the administration off Sturt's shoulders; and in 1894, Sturt consoled himself with the thought that a successful application would have meant having to move up to London, leaving the Farnham region for the first time in his life. In short, if Sturt had had the confidence to rely on his writings as a sole source of income – the commentaries on Ruskin and Morris, the novels, and finally the book reviews for the literary journals – he would almost certainly have found some way of unloading the business.

But he lacked that confidence and, in time, he came to lack the commitment as well. Between 1885 and 1889, Sturt did contribute a series of articles to William Morris's journal *The Commonweal* – on craftsmanship and modern industrial methods, Ruskin's educational theories and life in the East End sweatshops – and he continually re-read Ruskin's *Fors Clavigera* to convince himself that he had been forced into the right decision when he stopped working as a schoolmaster; but, as Arnold Bennett never ceased to remind him, his heart did not seem to be in it any more. Day-to-day life in the wheelwright's shop was

slowly convincing him that both Ruskin and Morris had ideal-
ised the concept of 'craftsmanship' beyond all recognition: on 6
November 1892, he wrote in his *Journal* of 'these fantastic rever-
sions to old methods – so common nowadays – which seem to
aim at reviving traditions dead and gone. Take, for instance,
William Morris's "Kelmscott Press" series. I cannot help thinking that Morris's admiration for ancient work (no doubt very
admirable) has in some ways led him astray.' The trouble with
Morris's writings was that the author was fond of 'a sort of back-
ward looking, with a sense of meanness in our own lives. 'Tis a
secondhand nobility that we get, and the heroism that delights
us is not our own, but our ancestors'.' It was ironic, Sturt later
added, that one of the wealthiest men in England should spend
so much of his time manufacturing a 'visionary paradise' for
working men – the original champagne socialist: but at least
Morris had some practical experience of the crafts he admired,
which might explain why working men were prepared to listen
to him. Even the conviction Sturt had gleaned from the *Fors
Clavigera* – that 'man's only decent occupation was in handicraft' – was by the 1890s categorised as a 'Ruskinian absurdity'.

But there was one aspect of Ruskin's thought which continued to mean a great deal to the owner of the wheelwright's shop,
in such times of doubt, and that was his critique of the educational system. Indeed, Sturt never tired of his running battle
with the authorities at Farnham Art School – a battle which
seems to have been partly based on his reading of Ruskin. In

December 1890, he complained to the painting staff that there was too much emphasis on formal knowledge in their teaching – 'superior humbug' – and not enough on 'know-how' – 'pure-drawing' and 'the technicalities'. In November 1891, he suggested that the teaching of 'elements of pure design' had become hopelessly confused with the practical training of students through design. 'I wish to show the possibility of teaching *first* the elements of pure design, and then the limitations of applied design, leaving technicalities to be learned in a more practical way. And I would like to show how, in past days, design was (as I believe) handed down traditionally, as the making of wheels was handed down. But I have no proofs at hand.' The elements of pure design were the key, of course, but where 'technicalities' were concerned, there was no substitute for learning by doing; the mistake was to imagine that know-how could be taught directly from books.

From the evidence of the *Journal*, two passages in Ruskin's *Fors Clavigera* would have struck a distinct chord in Sturt at this time, apart from the general attack on reductionism which is contained in that collection. In the first, Ruskin is observing the behaviour of two American girls, in a railway carriage travelling from Venice to Verona. The girls are obviously wealthy, and have apparently enjoyed the advantages of the best 'enlightened philosophical education' that money could buy:

> …they were travelling through a district which, if any
> of the world, should touch the hearts and delight the

eyes of young girls. Between Venice and Verona! …
But they perceived … nothing but the flies and the
dust. They pulled down the blinds the moment they
entered the carriage, and then sprawled, and writhed,
and tossed among the cushions of it … Only one
sentence was exchanged, in the fifty miles, on the
subject of things outside the carriage (the Alps being
once visible from a station where they had drawn up
the blinds).

'Don't those snow-caps make you cool?'

'No – I wish they did.'

And so they went their way, with sealed eyes and
tormented limbs, their numbered miles of pain.

One of the main troubles with the Grammar School curriculum, wrote Sturt, was that it did not encourage the pupils to *use
their eyes*.

In the second passage, Ruskin is describing the cuckoo clock
on the wall of his nursery in Herne Hill:

I havn't the least notion how any such clock says
'Cuckoo', … and I don't know how a barrel-organ
produces music by being ground; nor what real function the pea has in a whistle. Physical sciences – all this
– of a kind which would have been boundlessly interesting to me … if only I had been taught it with due
immediate practice and enforcement of true manufacture, or, in pleasant Saxon, 'handiwork'. But there

> shall not be on St. George's estate, a single thing in the
> house which people don't know how to make...

One of the main problems in Farnham, wrote Sturt, was that the students would be encouraged to take too much of their everyday environment for granted, if formal knowledge and know-how continued to be confused in the School curriculum.

During the period covered by the manuscript *Journal*, from 1890 to the 1920s, Sturt never tired of these ideas – whatever he may have thought of other 'Ruskinian absurdities' – and he remained full of admiration for the reasons why Ruskin wrote them down. For the *Fors Clavigera* was compiled while Ruskin was Slade Professor of Fine Art at Oxford, 'as a byework to quiet my conscience, that I might be happy in ... my own proper life of Art-teaching, at Oxford and elsewhere.'

Meanwhile, back at the wheelwright's shop, Sturt was quick to realise that his inflated notions about the arts and crafts tended to put off the paying customers – he wrote all his early books under the pseudonym 'George Bourne', since 'I can fancy 'em saying of me "If he's writing novels, he isn't attending to his business." Quite true.'

Much of his time was spent 'picking up the business as best I could from the men' – eight skilled workmen or apprentices. From the start, the schoolmaster was acutely aware that he was an outsider, that there were certain 'mysteries' into which it was already too late for him to be initiated; looking back after thirty years, he concluded that these 'mysteries' could never be 'properly fathomed' by someone who expected too much of what he called 'bookish training':

> In the course of many years, many things became clear to me in theory, so that I could form a pretty good opinion whether or not a finished wheel had been well put together ... but there were mysteries about getting that finish which I never properly fathomed. Bookish training was too feeble to enter into these final secrets; evidently there was something more, only revealed to skilled hands and eyes after years of experiment. Precision eluded me: my eyes didn't see it ... Theory could tell near the matter, yet that was not enough for the son and grandson of an expert. It could easily detect where a fault had been made; and yet fail after all to find exactly what the fault was. I feel sometimes too ignorant about wheel-making to say anything at all about it ...

At the time, Sturt was often surprised to discover just how many of 'these secrets' had, in fact, originally been learned 'from the books'. Only in retrospect did he develop a clear separation in his mind, between 'bookish training' and experience in all aspects of a craft:

> The beauty of the day had tempted me out, and I was clipping the quick-hedge. Grover [the gardener and odd-job man] came, with basket and rake and hedge-gloves, to gather up the clippings, and we chattered on,

of his brother-in-law Will, amongst other things, and of traction engines. Will has been driving an engine, which takes one truck of 3000 bricks …

"How many load d'ye reckon that, then – more than 4 horse load, en't it?"

Grover made no effort to reckon, but said easily, "Yes. They reckons three hunder and fifty is a load, of these here wire-cut bricks. Four hunder of the old red bricks; and stock bricks is five hunder. And slates, countless slates – they be twenty by ten – six hunder o' they goes to a load."

Here I commented on the endless varieties of technical knowledge, never dreamt of by people like myself; and Grover assented, without interest in me, or people or anything but his subject. "That's one o' the things you wants to learn, if you be goin' with hosses – When you get a load. Law! half o' these donknow whether they got a load or whether they en't. I've almost forgot now; but I learnt it, once."

"How d'ye mean 'learnt' it? Picked it up, I spose?"

"No – 'tis in a book. You can learn to reckon things." (I haven't got this exact by any means) If you be goin' for a tree, or a block of stone, or bricks, you wants to know what's a load for a hoss, or two or three hoss load. A mason told me once, when I was goin' for a block o' stone. He put his tape round it, and told me

> near the matter what it weighed. He said you always
> ought to carry a two foot rule in your pocket; and then
> put it across the stone – or praps tis two or three bits
> you got to take....

One of the reasons why Sturt found it difficult to enter the world of his craftsmen was that he felt obliged to master *all* the various activities which went on in the shop, whereas his employees were specialists in only one aspect of their trade. 'Of course I had far too many irons in the fire – that was one part of the trouble. I was trying to learn four or five trades at once; and "intellect" fooled me by making them look simple. Indeed, so much of handwork as intellect can understand does have that appearance, almost always to the undoing of the book-learned, who grow conceited. How simple is coal-hewing, fiddling, fishing, digging, to the student of books! I thought my business looked easy.' Although the schoolmaster reckoned that it was his 'intellect' alone which let him down, he had only to re-read William Morris to find a much more substantial reason – the detailed division of labour which existed even before the factory age.

Another reason was that he had not done his time as an apprentice, and as a result had become accustomed to a rather different occupation.

> Could not Intellect achieve it? In fact, Intellect made
> but a fumbling imitation of real knowledge, yet
> hardly deigned to recognise how clumsy in fact it was.

> Beginning so late in life I know now I could never
> have earned my keep as a skilled workman. But with
> the ambition to begin at the beginning I set myself …
> to act as a boy to any of the men who might want a
> boy's help.

Again, Sturt could not resist blaming his 'intellect' – when he had only to re-read John Ruskin to find colourful descriptions of specialisation and training in the crafts.

A third reason – one that Sturt found very difficult to accept in the beginning – was that he was the boss, and the wheelwrights were working for him. They clearly found his eager presence in the shop distracting (or sometimes amusing, 'not thinking I should see them smile') and quickly understood that his interests in the business were very different from their own – despite his affection for the work they were doing.

> They possibly (and properly) exaggerated the respect
> for good workmanship and material; and I cannot
> blame them if they slowed down in pace … To make it
> pay – that was not their affair … The time came when
> I found it needful to curb their own extravagance,
> scheming all sorts of ways, for instance, to get three
> shafts out of a plank, where a too fastidious workman
> would have cut only two….

In time, Sturt managed to master some aspects of the trade – he became pretty good with saw and plane, for example, after a clumsy start – but, where most of them were concerned, the men 'could not put into my wrist the knack that ought to have begun growing there five years earlier'.

'The nature of this knowledge should be noted,' he wrote in 1921 in *The Wheelwright's Shop*.

> It was set out in no book. It was not scientific. I never met a man who professed any other than an empirical acquaintance with the waggon-builder's law. My own case was typical. I know that the hind-wheels had to be five feet two inches high and the forewheels four feet two; that the "sides" must be cut from the best four-inch heart of oak, and so on. This sort of thing I knew, and in vast detail in course of time; but I seldom knew why. And that is how most other men knew.
>
> Reasoned science for us did not exist. 'Theirs is not to reason why.' What we had to do was to live up to the local wisdom of our kind; to follow the customs, and work to the measurements, which had been tested and corrected long before our time in every village shop all across the country … Science? Our two-foot rules took us no nearer to exactness than the sixteenth of an inch: we used to make or adjust special gauges for the nicer work, but very soon a stage was reached when eye and hand were left to their own cleverness, with no guide to help them. So the work was more of an art – a very fascinating art – than a science … A good wheelwright felt it, in his bones. It was a perception

> with him. But there was no science in it; no reasoning.
> Every detail stood by itself, and had to be learnt either
> by trial and error or by tradition.

Confronted by this knowledge, by what modern sociologists of science call 'a black box', Sturt's first temptation was to mythologise it, to put it on a pedestal, and pay homage to it in terms which meant a great deal to him: 'the artist's way', 'work as an art', 'a knowledge as valid as any artist's', 'real knowledge', 'the unconscious process', 'the mysteries'. Later, when he became more disillusioned with the sentimentality of the arts and crafts people and when he gave some thought to the problem of how the wheelwrights actually learned their trade (''tis in a book' – sometimes), he seems to have realised that his search for a suitably mysterious metaphor was in fact an attempt to cover up a basic confusion in his mind between two distinct types of knowledge – and, while it might say a lot about him (and about his tendency to retrospective regret), it said very little about the work of the wheelwrights. On the other hand there was the information which *could* be described to him in detail, which he could observe in action, which he could read about, and which, in principle, he could acquire whether he was in the wheelwright's shop or not – notably information about the use of specific tools, and about how to measure. The reason why he did not understand this information all at once was, of course, because the process took time – and probably because he approached it in the wrong frame of mind, rather like the lady who went up to Einstein at a cocktail party, asked him 'What exactly *are* your books about?' and was surprised when she got a short answer. This type of knowledge might be difficult to grasp – especially for an outsider – but it could be articulated and, with time and patience, it could be communicated as well. The other type of knowledge was, by contrast, made up entirely of tacit rules and understandings which were impossible to articulate in a formal way, simply because they only arose from the experience of living for a long time among a particular group of people, or what modern sociologists of science call 'an invisible college'.

The more Sturt tried to pin down *this* knowledge – to describe the tacit understandings and reduce them to a set of 'scientific' axioms – the more remote and complicated they seemed, and the more he was tempted to call them magic. Again, it was partly a matter of his frame of mind: he thought that he was after bits of information, or 'material' for his books, when in fact he was learning a kind of language. It was no use sitting in his study to learn it, agonising about whether or not it had anything to do with 'art' – there was no substitute for spending a lot of time working in the wheelwright's shop, until these tacit understandings became second nature to *him* as well. At first, Sturt thought that the wheelwrights were deliberately keeping information from him, that they were too inarticulate to tell – anything to explain why so much seemed strange to the schoolmaster. What particularly irked him was that 'one of the ablest, most intelligent men in my shop could not read or write,' but, he added, this man was 'versed in village lore; had begun at seven years old and picked up the rudiments of his trade in a country smithy'. And *there* was the answer. It was not a matter of whether or not the wheelwrights were articulate – for this type of knowledge was not articulable in that sense at all. It was a matter of learning the rules by living them.

Of course, the language which Sturt uses, when trying to draw attention to the mysteries of this particular 'black box', seems rather archaic today: he has a less than subtle notion of what a 'reasoned science' is, and tends to express his problems in terms of some very simple contrasts – between 'intellect' and 'real knowledge', 'bookish training' and 'a fascinating art'. This language has sometimes led design theorists to reappraise *The Wheelwright's Shop* exclusively in terms of its contribution to the development of the 'reasoned science' of design; in other words, to stress the significance of the *formal knowledge* contained in the book. Nigel Cross, for example, in his Open University book *Design and Technology*, considers that the reason why the 'waggon-builder's lore' was 'set out in no book' was simply that 'books and scientific knowledge require, at the very least, literacy, and probably training in, for example, the reading and making of technical drawings. These things require access to a formalised education system, which the craftsmen did not have.' J. Christopher Jones, in his article *Traditional and Modern Design Methods*, concludes that 'unlike the craftsmen who transmitted these forms without ever understanding the reasons for them, Sturt enquired the reasons' and came up with something resembling today's 'scientific method', in particular 'analysis of requirements and synthesis of logical solutions'. There are, admittedly, some passages in the book when Sturt's search for a type of knowledge which can be expressed by means of what he calls 'scientific' axioms may make him seem like a modern researcher – but it would have required something of a Damascus Road experience to convert this ex-disciple of Ruskin into a card-carrying supporter of the systematic design methods movement.

A few entries in the *Journal* suggest that Sturt was working towards an analysis of the distinction between the two types of knowledge – as he vaguely understood it – in terms of 'the present economic system' and the division between social classes which sustained the system: the skill and prowess of the labourer, he wrote, could 'fill his whole being with a subtle satisfaction; so that his day's work is to him what golf is to the idle "gentleman". There is more skill in it, probably, than in golf, and more variety; it involves far more knowledge and to this extent the man's life is better worth living than many a "gentleman's".' The gentleman was better educated, in formal terms, and was powerful enough to ensure that the labourer would always be the 'servant of industry' – but, in the end, the labourer's 'satisfaction in his labour is altogether more solid than the golfer's satisfaction in his play', and it may be that the gentleman's *only* skilled activity

– in craft terms – is the playing of a round of golf. Sturt was well aware of the dangers of this argument: 'I will not, dare not, say this in public, for fear of providing "gentlemen" with an excuse for preserving the present economic system': and he was by no means convinced that the argument was 'true enough'. But, as he sought a way of describing the process of 'learning the trade' without recourse to either the imagery of 'art' *or* the imagery of 'science', he tried a variety of different theoretical approaches including social analysis – without ever formulating any one of them in a systematic way.

In fact, the distinction between formal knowledge and tacit knowledge – expressed from a social, as well as a technical perspective – has only been clearly formulated in recent years, following developments in the philosophy of knowledge (during the 1960s) and the sociology of science (during the 1970s):

> When we think of material objects produced by handicraft rather than by mass-production, we easily appreciate the distinctive features of this sort of work. The craftsman works with particular objects; he must know their properties in all their particularity; and his knowledge of them cannot be specified in a formal account. Indeed, no explicit description of a crafts-man's techniques, and of the objects on which he works, can be more than the simplest elements of the subject. They can be useful for the beginner, but he must develop a personal, tacit knowledge of his objects

and what he can do with them, if he is to produce good work....

This distinction – presented here by a sociologist of *science*, Jerome Ravetz in his *Scientific Knowledge and its Social Problems* – between 'an explicit description' and 'a personal, tacit knowledge' is partly about expertise, partly about the experience of living and working in a particular culture, among an 'invisible college' of fellow practitioners, and it is intended to apply equally to craftspeople and scientists. Sturt became aware of its value, in his impressionistic way, as he tried to re-describe his experience of thirty years in *The Wheelwright's Shop*. But he never quite managed to bring it into focus, or to settle his point of view. As he wrote in his *Journal* at the end of 1904:

> … in relation to an essay which will not 'come', dealing with the technical knowledge of labouring people. Here and there in application (as in steering a boat to a quay, or driving a team of horses round a corner) the working man's knowledge and judgement give results that arrest all eyes, so that all easily find them 'beautiful'. But for the most part (and wholly when taken in aggregate) the fitness of this knowledge eludes me. My present feeling is, of being just on the point of perceiving it; there is the 'raw material' of it, merely waiting for me to alter my focus a little or shift my point of view, when all will be plain. But I get no farther, and the true subject of my article is therefore still to seek.

Ironically, given the schoolmaster's strong views on the differences between 'knowledge' and 'know-how' in art and design education, he had confused the two himself – and in the process of sorting out the confusion, was 'just on the point of perceiving' one of the key insights in the modern sociology of knowledge.

Only when he had arrived at this realisation – however vaguely – could Sturt muster the confidence to write *The Wheelwright's Shop*, for it enabled him to lay bare some of the processes by which he had gathered his knowledge and information, and so to anchor his work in a central problem – 'learning the trade'. In one sense, the book would have been much easier to write some thirty years before, when the schoolmaster still trusted the abstractions of Ruskin and Morris, and still subscribed to the myth of the happy artisan. For, at first he had had to rely on this frame of reference, in order to make the behaviour of the men, the work they did, and the local 'Farmer Tupps' for whom they worked all seem less remote – but eventually he came to reject it. The frame simply did not fit the picture.

In another sense, the book would have been easier to write – far easier – if Sturt's aim had been to outline the formal design principles embodied 'unselfconsciously' in the work of 'craftsmen who transmitted these forms without ever understanding the reason for them' until the schoolmaster came along. At one stage during the drafting of the book, he seems to have planned a more descriptive technical account of the ways in which the wheelwrights went about solving their design problems: as part of his research in 1921 he drew a series of diagrams of the workmen's tools, carefully listing their technical properties and making some tentative suggestions as to their capabilities. But, by the time he wrote the final text, his interest had shifted to the type of knowledge which was 'set out in no book', and which could never be reduced to the axioms of what he called 'reasoned science'. The main point about this knowledge, for Sturt, was not that it was 'unselfconscious' – on the contrary it was often based on 'laws as inevitable as gravitation', sometimes took the concrete form of 'patterns' or jigs which the wheelwrights inherited, and was still protected, in other trades, by the guild structure – but that after nearly forty years of what today's social scientists would consider 'participant observation' the schoolmaster could only profess 'an empirical acquaintance' with it. Sturt's interest in this type of knowledge was expressed in his emphasis on the 'skill' and 'experience of every difficulty' with which the workmen's tools were used (rather than on the technical properties of the tools); in the many instances he cites of the wheelwrights' adaptability to new problems (most notably the fitting of solid metal tyres); in his cynicism about how far 'bookish training' could take him; and above all in his nostalgia for the world we have lost. The concept of an 'unselfconscious process' only makes sense if we accept the modern distinction between someone called a 'designer' and someone called a 'maker' (or, to put it in a Ruskinian way which the schoolmaster would have recognised, between 'one man who is always thinking and another who is always working'): such a distinction had never existed in the wheelwright's shop, and as he looked back Sturt was critical of the social and economic pressures which had forced him, reluctantly, to come to terms with it.

The moral of the tale – where both the schoolmaster and the wheelwrights are concerned – is clear enough. Only when the schoolmaster had shed both his 'Ruskinian tendencies' *and* his tendency to rely on the reassuring categories of 'reasoned science' did he even begin to understand the work and society of the craftsmen, and did they begin to understand what he was attempting to do.

George Sturt always thought of the book as a requiem for the wheelwrights, a way of ensuring that history would not forget them. But *The Wheelwright's Shop* offers a great deal more than that: it offers a way of writing that history, it stimulates reflection on that history, and it succeeds in helping us make sense of that over-used and much abused term 'craftsmanship'.

# 2. Forever Ambridge

O N THE COVER of Martin Wiener's book *English Culture and the Decline of the Industrial Spirit* (1981, paperback 1983), there is a reproduction of Ford Madox Brown's mid-Victorian painting of *Work*: a small group of artisans poses heroically on a building site in Hampstead, while two philosophers stand nearby, presumably conducting an informal seminar on the moral value of good old English craftsmanship. It is an appropriate image, for Martin Wiener's book is about a range of social and cultural reactions to the process of industrialisation in this country, from the 1850s to the present day, and specifically about the inability (or unwillingness) of the British elite in the modern period to come to terms with the implications of technological change. There is, as he suggests, some corner of the English mind that is forever Ambridge.

Wiener's main argument is that although England was the first country in the world to go through the trauma of industrialisation, providing a model for all other advanced economies to emulate, England never really industrialised *culturally*. The first wave of industrialists – the entrepreneurs, the iron masters, the engineers, the political economists – may have written enthusiastically about economic growth, technological change, and the benefits of material progress: at that stage in our cultural history,

Samuel Smiles (the most popular writer of moral tales about 'the industrial spirit') could ask, 'What is England without its tools, its machinery, its steam-engine, its steam-ships and its locomotives? Are not the men who have made the motive power of the country, and immensely increased its productive strength, the men who have above all made the country what it is?' But something happened to that enthusiasm, and to the moral of the tales, in the decade of the Great Exhibition, a decade which began with the construction of the Crystal Palace and ended with the deaths of the three giants of British engineering: Isambard Brunel, Robert Stephenson, and Joseph Locke. For, just as Paxton's iron and glass construction had contained within it Pugin's Medieval Court – a bizarre expression of its cultural opposite – so a succession of novelists, politicians, artists and designers began systematically to construct an alternative vision of England to set against the industrial values of the previous generation. In the process, they succeeded in accommodating, or domesticating, the Industrial Revolution, to suit an aristocratic *and* bourgeois elite which had no wish to confront its cultural implications. Hence the invention of 'Coketown' as an image of the dark, satanic North, and the invention of 'Merrie England' as an image of the green and pleasant South. The young William Morris refused to go into the Crystal Palace, and preferred to sit outside.

This alternative vision – representing a *critical* tradition, in contrast to the *normative* tradition of the first half of the century

– might not have had much effect on our economic performance, had it not been accompanied and reinforced by a series of social changes and new social institutions, dating from the latter half of the nineteenth century. Martin Wiener provides a long list of them: the rise of the public schools, with their rejection of science and technology as significant parts of the curriculum; the rise of the new universities, with their emphasis on 'classical' academic subjects, Oxbridge-style; the rise of the art and design colleges, which were founded to train designers for manufacturing industry, but which rapidly turned into finishing schools for fine artists and 'fine art workmen'; the rise of the professions (such as law, medicine and architecture) which provided a new career path for the first sons of industrialists and the second sons of the landowning aristocracy; and the gentrification of successful members of the middle class, whose ambition it became to settle down in 'the countryside' (another new invention) rather than invest the family fortune in risky industrial ventures. Running through all these social developments, like a fine tweed, was a fairy-tale image of Englishness which was based on traditional peace and quiet, gentility, and something called the quality of life – an image which was made tangible in the conservation movement (evidence, perhaps, of a loss of confidence in the creative powers of one's industrial contemporaries) and which has lasted well into the twentieth century. Mr Toad may flirt with the new technology, but Ratty, Mole and Badger are always there to bring him back to his senses.

According to Martin Wiener, the standard *economic* explanations of Britain's poor industrial performance for much of the twentieth century have all been tried and found wanting. Has economic growth been held back by cyclical fluctuations caused by stop-go financial policies? In fact, the relationship between economic cycles and growth has in the period in question been less dramatic in Britain than elsewhere. Has low investment been the reason? In the relevant historical periods, he says, investment in Britain was just as high as in other countries. Has Britain suffered from unfavourable terms of trade? Only sometimes. Has government spending been too high? It has been, he argues, no higher than in more successful countries. Has heavy taxation discouraged entrepreneurial initiative? Britain stands roughly in the middle of the world league table of overall taxation. By the same, or a similar token, purely economic explanations of our long-term economic retardation have, for Wiener, proved to be inadequate:

> the classical factors of supply – capital, labour and natural resources – by themselves explain little. Late-Victorian and Edwardian Britain boasted capital resources unprecedented in world history, resources adequate to support continued economic leadership. Charles Kindleberger of MIT concluded after a careful study of the period from 1851 to 1950 that "by any reasonable test the supply of British capital was sufficient". The size and competence of Britain's labour

force posed no obvious obstacles to growth. There was neither a shortage of labour nor such a surplus as to discourage industrial investment. Supplies of the chief industrial resources – coal, iron and other minerals – were more than adequate to maintain vigorous expansion. It was, as Kindleberger concluded, the *use* made of resources, of labour and of capital that was crucial.

Wiener's conclusion to all this – and it is a seductive one – is that a wider approach to the problem of our economic decline is required, an approach which takes into full account both social structure and culture. Development economists – such as Gunnar Myrdal in his monumental *Asian Drama* – have long recognised the importance of cultural history as part of an explanation of economic performance in Third World countries. It has even been suggested (much to the fury of some economic historians) that 'rational economic behaviour' depends to a large extent on the social and cultural context. Martin Wiener is simply applying this analytical method to the oldest industrial nation in the world. In his scenario, Britain's economic decline has a lot to do with 'the decline of the industrial *spirit*' – a unique cultural phenomenon, he says, which has been both reinforced by, and symptomatic of, changes in the social structure (notably a split in the middle class).

When *English Culture and the Decline of the Industrial Spirit* was first published it had the unusual distinction of being reviewed, and favourably, by a Marxist historian and by *Country*

*Life* both at the same time. Tom Nairn, in the *Guardian*, reckoned that the book provides 'a much more reliable ideological chart of modern Englishness than any previous cultural history, and does so coolly and persuasively'. A *Country Life* review, written by an anonymous 'countryman', waxed lyrical about Weiner's account of 'the cultural ideals which this weekly magazine attempts to represent' – a rather surprising achievement for an American. But Tom Nairn was less happy with the book's social analysis: for, as he pointed out, even if many successful entrepreneurs did retire to their country houses, and did choose to engage in more 'gentlemanly' pursuits than industry and trade (such as hunting, shooting and fishing), they never for a moment turned their backs on *capitalism*. 'The decline of the industrial spirit,' he goes on, 'has been accompanied by the consistent vitality and ascendancy of other forms of the capitalist spirit. The rundown of engineering, Crystal Palace England was the rejuvenation of traditional, mercantile England; it was the promotion of the City and Sterling to being the indispensable hub of the developing world market. This was the real "tradition" which furnished the positive momentum for false archaism, anti-industrial foamings and gentrification.' It could be argued, however, that the world of the stock exchange – with its traditions of gambling, of 'bulls and bears' – is quite close to the myth of the Regency English gentleman sitting at the gaming table, so Tom Nairn's point about the City may be accommodated, just about, within the Martin Wiener thesis. Certainly, our national propensity to make folk-heroes out of business-men-gamblers who take huge risks and then go spectacularly bust and to ignore businessmen who operate with more success and less flamboyance, would suggest that gambling for very high stakes, whether at Newmarket, in the City, or at Gatwick Airport, can sometimes overcome the stigmas of 'being in trade', in this strange culture of ours.

The conclusion to Martin Wiener's book can be read in two very distinct ways: the book is *either* a kind of funeral sermon, to be read as the decaying corpse of British manufacturing is sent on its final journey; *or* it predicts that Britain may well be in the vanguard of 'post-industrialism', and peculiarly well-equipped to cope with a future of increasing 'leisure' and wide-spread automation assuming that is what is to happen. If we accept the former conclusion, then we must also accept that 'it is no longer a matter of growing more slowly than other econo-mies, or even of "zero-growth", but rather a matter of *negative* growth, of "de-industrialisation". This is a cost greater than the British, I think, are prepared to pay'; the only solution, accord-ing to Wiener, is to drag our society and culture kicking and screaming into the twentieth century. If, on the other hand, we accept the latter conclusion (like economists in the school of Professor J.K. Galbraith), we can calmly reassure ourselves that 'the short-circuiting of the Industrial Revolution in the cultural realm has, at the same time as retarding economic development, also buttressed a number of attractive features of British life

– political stability (at least until very recently), and certainly environmental concern and appreciation of the value of leisure'. Predictably enough, *Country Life* prefers to look on the bright side: 'could it not be that the traditional values, which Professor Wiener thinks are our undoing, will in the end prove to be our continuing strength?'

*English Culture and the Decline of the Industrial Spirit* is an uneven book – far stronger on cultural, than on economic or social history. It tends to present a monolithic picture of 'industry', when most of the recent researches suggest that Britain's industrial development in the nineteenth century occurred in an altogether more haphazard way: the workshop of the world, it now seems, depended to great extent on hand work and steam power, except in those few areas of the economy where manufacture had given way to machinofacture. It does not emphasise enough the importance of Imperial territories as captive dumping-grounds for English products. But it is a helpful and important book nonetheless, which even contains some hard lessons for those of us with a professional interest in craft and design – both in the past and in the present. The central thesis helps to explain why we are so much better at setting up quangos and professional organisations, than we are at remedying the historical *and* contemporary mismatch between design and (what's left of) manufacturing industry. It also helps to explain our enduring fascination with the *mythology* of craftsmanship – the myth of the happy artisan, the myth of paradise lost, and the myth – against all the evidence – that craftsmanship is an exclusively rural occupation. It provides a long-term geneal-ogy for the debate (which has been going on at least since the 1850s) about the proper role of design education: the debate is as heated and unresolved as ever it was; only the elegance of expression has been lost. And, perhaps most of all, Martin Wiener's book can help us to understand the complex reaction of English culture to the arrival of the new technologies (and their attendant imagery) – a reaction which has embraced home computers and video machines with open arms, so long as they remain a leisure activity, but which where industrial production is concerned still seems to prefer William Morris, artist-crafts-man, to the other one. *Plus ça change...*?

# 3. Skill – a word to start an argument

IN RECENT YEARS the words 'crafted' and 'hand-built' have become absorbed into the language of advertising and packaging, and into popular culture in general. We see these words and the rural imagery usually associated with them all over the place – promoting everything from cars, processed foods, new housing developments and building societies to wristwatches, cigarettes, beers and clothes. The phenomenon has become so widespread that a recent survey of the state of the language devoted a whole section to the word 'crafted' as one of those words in everyday vocabulary which 'beguile as well as inform'. 'When advertising people use "crafted" as a substitute for "manufactured"', the survey went on, 'they are attempting to delude the public into believing that something has been made by hand in a carefully old-fashioned way.' The hoardings do not actually say this – they simply smuggle it in. Hence the slogan 'hand-built by robots' and its rival 'more space, more craft', in which the reassuring connotations of 'hand-built' and 'craft' are calculated to offset the less-reassuring connotations of robots and space-age technology.

Craft is trustworthy, microchips are not – at least, not yet. It is as if the advertisers are selling our own nostalgia back to us at a profit. Perhaps the campaign that has made the fullest use of this strategy is the series of 45-second films promoting Hovis on television. By means of this campaign some mass-produced goods are associated in consumers' minds with brass bands in rural Yorkshire during the early part of this century, bakeries run by early craftsmen and their even more elderly apprentices, technicolour villages of the mind to beguile the supermarket shopper into believing that it is as good today as it has always been. If the strategy works – and it seems to, even if it does create problems when you are trying to launch a new product – it says a lot about the continuing potency of 'craft' as an idea. Assembly lines may be manned by robots. The corner grocery shop may long since have been demolished. Convenience foods may seem too processed for comfort, at least for some of us. But the advertisers can rely on the simple word 'crafted' to relieve for a moment the complex anxieties which these social and economic processes have created.

Of course, the word 'crafted' is not confined to the billboards, and the ad men did not conjure this imagery out of thin air. As a result of the recent 'craft revival' (as it has been called), the word can be seen wherever there is a corn-dolly or a bean-bag, wherever Janey Morris look-alikes walk around in their new Laura Ashley frocks, wherever pine is stripped, wherever souvenir shops have changed their names to craft shops, and wherever post-Glastonbury hippies congregate to sing about what they imagine it was like before the war memorial took over from the maypole in the village square. Confronted by these disconnected bits of the olde worlde, we may well be tempted to echo the drunken sentiments of Lucky Jim:

> The point about *Merrie England* is that it was about the most un-Merrie period in our history. It's only the homemade pottery crowd, the organic husbandry crowd, the recorder playing crowd who…

In other words, there's not much use in being a 'homecomer' unless we know exactly what or where 'home' is.

Lucky Jim's famous lecture – dealing as it did with the 'integration of social consciousness' and the 'identification of work with craft' – was intended, in part, as a satire on the style of literary history (just as fashionable in the early nineteen-fifties as it is today) which was really a sustained lament for 'the world we have lost', a history in which today's synthetic, entrepreneurial culture is always compared unfavourably with the culture of yesterday's 'organic community'. In pointing out that the 'organic community' of old England never really existed, that it is always 'over the last hill', Raymond Williams has recently drawn attention to an unbroken chain of 'retrospective regret' for an age which had just passed – and which was usually thought to have been on its last legs during the childhood of the writer. Williams's *The Country and the City* shows how this unbroken chain leads from John Betjeman (in our time), via F.R. Leavis, George Sturt and Thomas Hardy, all the way back to Oliver Goldsmith's *Deserted Village* in 1769 – and probably beyond that to the Garden of Eden. Where the world of the craftsman is concerned, we can construct our own parallel chain of 'retrospective regret', which leads from, say, Edward Barnsley, via Ernest Gimson and C.R. Ashbee in the Cotswolds, and Eric Gill and Ethel Mairet in Ditchling, to William Morris, thence to a Sussex furniture-maker named Ephraim Coleman and, by a huge imaginative leap, to Merrie England in the reign of Edward I. Williams's purpose is not to condemn such nostalgia out of hand, but to look closely at 'each kind of retrospect as it comes' in order to understand when *la mode rétro* is a strategy for criticising the present, and when it is simply an escape from the present.

The recent 'craft revival' is clearly based on a certain reading of English history, using evidence of the aesthetic (as well as moral and ritual) value of certain English artefacts from the past as evidence of how these artefacts must have been both produced and consumed. It is implicitly based on a series of contrasting images – between 'the craftsman' and 'the industrial worker', 'doing is designing' and 'thinking is designing', 'happy artisans' and 'unhappy machine-minders'. Robert Blauner in his influential writings on *Work Satisfaction and Industrial Trends* has commented on some of these contrasts, which lie hidden at the centre of many a history of craftsmanship:

> It is remarkable what an enormous impact this contrast of the craftsman with the factory hand has had on intellectual discussions of work and workers in modern society, notwithstanding its lack of corre-

spondence to present and historical realities. For, indeed, craftsmen, far from being typical workers of the past era, accounted for less than ten per cent of the medieval labour force, and the peasant, who was actually the representative labourer, was … practically nothing more than a working beast.… In modern society there is far greater scope for skill and craftsmanship than in any previous society.

Perhaps the most obvious example of how historically misleading these contrasts can be is provided by the contemporary image and status of the craft potter who sees himself as the inheritor of traditional skills. For, although craft pottery is today the most popular of handicrafts, it played a negligible part in the urban economy of Merrie England. The Guilds do not seem to have given any protection to clay potters (since there was very little demand for their products in the towns) and when clay was worked by medieval craftsman, it was mainly to produce tiles and bricks for those who could not afford stone. Only in the countryside, where neither the work nor the products were subject to Guild inspection, did potters spend a significant proportion of their time serving the domestic needs of the local community by making vessels for the kitchen or the peasant's hut. From the sixteenth century onwards, this kind of production was mainly based in small workshops and rural households. As the family economy (which continued what there was of the medieval 'craft' tradition) became linked through merchant investment with the capitalist organisation of trade, putting-out, and the marketing of products, 'proto-industrial families' developed more and more extreme methods of unregulated self-exploitation in the production of craft goods. Eventually, according to the most recent researches, they managed in times of scarcity to sustain a work output 'even beyond the amount which is customary in an economic system depending on developed capitalist wage labour', a primitive kind of mass production of handicrafts. The myth of the happy artisan – like the 'artist craftsman', craft guilds to which select potters could belong, and the confusion of rural workers with guild craftsman – did not exist until the nineteenth century, when it became part of a romantic reaction against the spread of industrial capitalism. And the history which underpins much of the 'craft revival' is, in fact, nostalgia masquerading as history.

All this has now become a fashion, and it has been going on at a time when commercial publishing has come to depend on illustrated reprints of nostalgic reminiscences about the rural world we have lost. It is perhaps significant that many of these books, such as Flora Thompson's *Lark Rise to Candleford* and the books of folk songs selected by Vaughan Williams, originally date from the agricultural depression of the 1920s, another period of dislocation. A glance at the best-seller lists shows that this fashion for retrospective regret has been commercially stable over at least the past decade. In books ranging from *The Diary of an Edwardian Lady* to the *AA Book of British Villages* we have been offered the countryside of the pre-First World War as static object to be viewed through a car window — disconnected and gift-wrapped bits of a previous culture. When they were written, the books by Flora Thompson and the Edwardian Lady may have represented a continuity of experience from the 1880s through to the 1920s. Today they do not.

Another good example of the way in which the fashion for *la mode rétro* can distort the history it is exploiting is the pervasive use of the Saxony spinning wheel as a key symbol of the domestic crafts. This symbol can be seen in the windows of many 'craft' shops and on the logos of craft organisations. Victorian photographs and watercolours of spinning wheels in drawing rooms, or of young ladies engaging in a spot of home spinning, appear to reinforce the association. No one seems to have noticed that it is rather odd for a late-fifteenth-century piece of technology to be in general domestic use in the mid-nineteenth century at a time when spinning machines — starting with Hargreaves's jenny, Arkwright's wheel and Crompton's mule — had been around for some seventy years, and when the skilled handicraft end of the trade used the great wheel rather than the Saxony wheel. It is odd but quite explicable when we think of the Saxony wheel as a piece of furniture rather than as a piece of technology: a great wheel would have looked distinctly odd in a Victorian drawing room. It is further explained by recalling that the fashion for home spinning in Victorian times had much more to do with the desire of second-generation industrialists to pretend their wealth had nothing to do with industry, than (except in some isolated cases) with the genuine survival of a craft. So the Victorian spinning wheel, about which we are encouraged to be so nostalgic, was to a large extent nostalgic in the first place, a symbol of status rather than of craft survival. And a way of 'making things' as a leisure occupation.

Now such popular images of craft and workmanship – from 'hand-built by robots' to the spinning wheel – may seem very remote from the world of the craft teacher or indeed from the world of the practising craftsman today. However, I believe that sensible arguments in support of the crafts in education and society – arguments for the benefit of educators, civil servants, grant-givers of all descriptions, sponsors, and society at large – are in danger of being confused with less sensible arguments, based as they are on a mixture of sentiment, bad history, and a misunderstanding of the lessons of the Arts and Crafts Movement. And it is of crucial importance to separate the two. There *are* hard-edged arguments, but it's not always easy to dismiss the popular connotations of the crafts. We have to live with them: the crafts as folksy, alternative, rural occupations associated with a homecoming vision of the future, and also with a nostalgia masquerading as history. For these connotations represent the most powerful perspective on craft in the late twentieth century that there is, backed as it is by advertising, commercial publishing, the record industry, and even some colleges of art and design where, regrettably, the look of the

Arts and Crafts Movement was made orthodox while its social philosophy was abandoned.

I shall not presume to look at the contemporary crafts in terms of educational theory because I think that Robert Witkin, in his *Intelligence of Feeling*, has already presented a persuasive defence of the role of craft, as distinct from art, education in the development of what he calls 'the inner world of sensations and feelings', and in particular the crucial role of *action* in an individual child's balanced development. Witkin's conclusion is that since most of the children covered by his pioneering survey wanted to be free to express themselves *and* to work within reassuring guidelines at the same time, and since they were lukewarm in their response to art classes as being too free of rules to meet these objectives, the craft subjects represent the best available means of developing the intelligence of feeling. His conclusion does not need restating here, but one of Witkin's philosophical distinctions does lead directly to my first perspective on craft: it is a distinction between types of knowing. Perhaps the best way of introducing this distinction is to retell a famous story and to add a gloss on it provided by a distinguished American psychologist. It is entitled 'Never know when it might come in useful', and I think it is from the ancient Persian:

> Nasrudin sometimes took people for trips in his boat. One day a pedagogue hired him to ferry him across a wide river. As soon as they were afloat the scholar asked whether it was going to be rough. "Don't ask

me nothing about it," said Nasrudin. "Have you never studied grammar?" "No." "In that case, half your life has been wasted." Nasrudin said nothing. Soon a terrible storm blew up. Nasrudin's crazy cockleshell was filling with water. He leaned over towards his companion. "Have you ever learned to swim?" "No," said the pedant. "In that case, schoolmaster, *all* your life has been wasted, for we are sinking."

As Robert Ornstein notes in *The Psychology of Consciousness* (1972):

> The two characters in this story represent two major modes of consciousness. The verbal rational mode is portrayed by the pedagogue who's involved in and insists on neat and tidy perfection. The other mode is represented by the skill of swimming, which involves movement of the body in space, a mode often devalued by the neat rational mind of the pedagogue. On one level these two characters represent different types of people. The verbal logical grammarian can also be the scientist, the logician, the mathematician who is committed to reason and correct proof. The boatman, ungraceful and untutored in formal terms, represents the craftsman, the dancer, the dreamer whose output is often unsatisfactory to the purely rational mind.

Now this distinction between the pedagogue and the boatman has been formulated in many different ways. Sometimes it has been a hard and fast distinction between knowing how and knowing what, between knowing how to do something and knowing a piece of information. Sometimes it has been presented as part of a continuing process which encompasses a whole spectrum – knowing what, knowing who, knowing when, knowing where, knowing why and knowing how. Sociologists distinguish between formal knowledge and tacit knowledge, the kind that can be found in books and is easily articulable, and the kind that cannot since it can never be articulated in verbal terms. The best example of this, which sociologists always use, is from Wittgenstein's description of people learning algebra, where he says that a person coming out of an algebra class can say: 'I learnt how to do equations … you cancel one side and then you cancel the other.' But what the person cannot say is that the equation was written on the blackboard, that it was written with chalk, that it means the same thing whether it was written with chalk or biro, and so on. In other words, *all* things that he takes for granted about the lesson in algebra he cannot really articulate because he cannot ever redescribe in words everything about what happened when he learnt something. The distinction is, of course, between the formal knowledge that is the algebraic equation and the tacit knowledge that is all the things that a person has experienced in the classroom by being socialised into the idea of being taught. It is a distinction which runs right through modern sociology and anthropology.

Design theorists distinguish between recipe knowledge, where an individual can never be sure of the outcome each time he or she acts upon it, and knowledge of principles, where it is assumed that individuals and even groups *can* be sure of outcomes. Philosophers distinguish between knowledge and know-how. The distinction was perhaps most forcefully expressed by Michael Oakeshott. Oakeshott expressed the fear that the educational system was becoming too geared to the transmission of what he called 'formal knowledge'. It was downgrading know-how at its peril – not because this could be directly linked to vocational training, which is the standard argument, but because it represented a way of knowing which was the most important for getting around in the world. He did not present his argument in terms of education *versus* training, but rather as education *through* training. Here is a characteristic example quoted from Oakeshott's *Rational Conduct* (collected in his *Rationalism in politics and other essays*, 1967):

> Doing anything both depends upon and exhibits knowing how to do it and though part but never the whole of knowing how to do it can subsequently be reduced to knowledge in the form of rules and principles, these propositions are neither the spring of the activity nor are they in any direct sense regulators of the activity. The characteristic of the carpenter in the ordinary conduct of life and his relations with other people and with the world is a knowledge not of certain

propositions about himself, his tools and the materials in which he works, but the knowledge of how to decide certain questions and this knowledge is a condition of the exercise of the power to construct propositions after the event... We may be agreed that it is preposterous to suppose an activity can spring from the premeditation of propositions about the activity but we are still apt to believe that in order to *teach* an activity, it is necessary to have converted our knowledge of it into a set of propositions: the grammar of a language; the rules of research; the principles of experiment; the canons of good workmanship – and that in order to learn an activity we should begin with such propositions... [B]ut it must be observed that not only are these rules an abridgement of the teacher's concrete knowledge of the activity and therefore after the activity itself, but learning them is never more than the meanest part of education in an activity. *They can be taught but they are not the only things that can be learnt from the teacher.* To work alongside a practised craftsman is an opportunity not only to learn the rules but to acquire also a direct knowledge of how he sets about his business and among other things a knowledge of how and when to apply the rules; and until this is acquired nothing of great value has been learned at all.

This important quotation neatly – some might say too neatly – states the knowledge/know-how distinction and it flies in the face of much modern educational theory, to say nothing of some contemporary practice in the art and craft world. The argument is part of a sustained explanation of what the concept of rationality means in everyday life, and it is radical in its implications even today: it has a slight 'either/or' feel to it which some philosophers and educationalists might question. But it still stands as a most clearly stated challenge to those who would wish to turn craft education towards more formal types of knowledge. The pressure was there when Oakeshott was writing, and it is certainly there today – with the current debate about 'crafts' versus 'design methods'. This, then, is my first major perspective on craft and skill.

My second one arises out of the first, and relates to the thorny question: What exactly is a skill? Most writings on craftsmanship, Oakeshott's included, make huge assumptions about the importance of skill, but there seems to be no general agreement about what the word means. Does it refer to manual dexterity, craft experience, conceptual activity, general know-how, or a shifting combination of these four? If the word means something different in each different kind of work, as some people have said, are any generalisations about skill possible? This is not just an academic question, for in the end most arguments about the crafts, in social terms at any rate, boil down to the value we attach to the exercise of what are known as 'certain skills'. Since practising artist-craftsmen are by no means agreed about this, some of them rejecting or downgrading manual skill or technique as a component in their creative work as artists, it is important that we try to find some common ground. Otherwise, it is possible that the art and craft world will increasingly cut loose from the assumptions which lie at the root of the crafts in education – assumptions about the coordination of perceptual and motor activity, or, to put this another way, of intellectual and manual work. I mean if an artist-craftsman who believes that his art has little or nothing to do with technical skill visits a school workshop, what exactly will be the benefit of his or her teaching by example? They may encourage children in their ambition to be artist superstars, but that is surely not the point. As David Pye has said, in recent years 'skill' has become a word to start an argument.

It may be necessary to re-examine the analysis by John Ruskin, William Morris and others of the degradation of work *in general* in the late nineteenth century, a tendency that has become known as 'deskilling', in order to find a more hard-edged use for the concept of skill in today's complex art and craft world. After all, the invention of the artist-craftsman or the fine-art workman was indirectly based on Ruskin's and Morris's analysis of skill. If there is any common ground perhaps it will emerge from the same sources. On the face of it, the Arts and Crafts line on deskilling in society at large remains persuasive. If we place a plate from Diderot's famous *Encyclopédie* published in the mid-eighteenth century (a picture of a small-scale manufactory) side by side with a late-nineteenth-century print (of a large machine-factory) the main difference is striking and obvious. In the former the artisan's relationship to the equipment is that of a musician to a musical instrument; in the latter the worker's relationship to the machine is that of a cog or lever.

The classic eighteenth-century example from the *Encyclopédie* is of a pin factory, and it is of some interest because Adam Smith used the example of a pin factory nearly twenty years later, in *The Wealth of Nations*, to illustrate his point about the division of labour required to produce an object as simple as a pin. If we look at the relationship of the figures to the equipment they are using, in the pin factory, they are involved and participating in the equipment – *even in the classic example of the division of labour*. And if we then look at the print of a hundred years later – say, of a vertical planing machine from the Soho Foundry in the 1860s – we can see that the relationship of the man to his machine is that of a working part. He stands alone, attending to it. The division of labour has developed since the days of the pin factory, and a new component has been added in the form of *automation*. Whereas the pin-makers exercised some control over the stage of the pin-making process for which they were responsible, the machine-minder has no control at all. And it is not just a question of 'machines' versus 'people', as some intellectual Luddites have suggested: it is more a question of *the ways in which the machines are used*, and of *the context for their use*.

The point is that if we read accounts of the traditional crafts at the time of the Industrial Revolution and compare them with accounts of similar activities written a hundred years later, the contrast seems to tell us a lot about the degradation of work which happened in the interim. The eighteenth-century craftsmen, as economic historian David Landes has written, were not on the whole the unlettered tinkers of historical mythology.

Even the ordinary millwright was usually a fair arithmetician, knew something of geometry, levelling and measuring and in some cases possessed a very competent knowledge of practical mathematics. He could calculate the velocities, strength and power of machines and could draw in plan and section.

By the end of the nineteenth century, however, or so the analysis of Ruskin and Morris goes, the separation of this kind of craft knowledge from craft skill was complete in most areas contributing significantly to the economy. Some contemporary, articulate critics of this separation thought they were clear as to the reasons why.

Here is one critic of the 1890s, writing about the deskilling tendency in the *International Moulders' Journal*:

> We think of craftsmanship ordinarily as the ability to manipulate skilfully the tools and materials of a craft or trade but true craftsmanship is much more than this. The really essential element in it is not manual skill and dexterity but something stored up in the mind of the worker. This something is partly the inti-

mate knowledge of the character and uses of the tools, materials and processes of the craft which tradition has given the worker but beyond this and above this, it is the knowledge which enables him to understand and overcome the constantly arising difficulties that grow out of variations, not only in tools and materials but in the conditions under which the work must be done.

Instead of this combination of knowledge and dexterity, the craftsman in industry is faced with the gathering up of all this scattered craft knowledge, systematising it and concentrating it in the hands of the employer and then doling it out again only in the form of minute instructions on how to be a machine minder, giving to each worker only the knowledge needed for the performance of a particular, relatively minute task. This process, it is evident, separates skill and knowledge even in their narrow relationship and when it is completed the worker is no longer a craftsman in any sense, but is an animated tool.

This is a very powerful thesis and, it seems to me, the foundation of much that Ruskin and Morris wrote about – in particular the role of the crafts in society as a very visible antidote. However, there are problems with this 'deskilling' thesis as an explanation of what had happened since the days of our ordinary millwright. But they are problems that can get us a little closer to agreeing what a skill really is. First of all, the thesis is based on a somewhat static notion of skill. According to Ruskin and Morris and many other subsequent writers about the degradation of work, skills tend to be lost forever rather than redistributed or redeployed or reformed. I return to this point shortly. Second, the thesis depends on the rather sentimental assumption that a whole range of pre-industrial activities like plain hand-loom weaving, the most famous example, were once highly skilled, when in fact some of them appear to have been almost as mechanical as the semi-automated activities which succeeded them.

Third, the thesis boldly contrasts something called 'craft' with something called 'industry' and tends to assume that more activities were highly automated in England than was in fact the case. Just after William Morris's death, the only areas which fitted this description – of machine-minders who had been utterly 'deskilled' – were large corporations producing soap, chemicals, foodstuffs, and textiles (Karl Marx's favourite example). Most current research into this history seems to be proving that hand-work and mass-production industries existed side by side into the late nineteenth century, and that the specifically English experience of industrialisation involved a close interaction of the two. So it was not simply a matter of industry taking over from craft, but of craft *within* industry – steam technology; hand work – throughout the nineteenth century. When Ruskin and Morris evolved their famous images of automated factory work in Victorian England they may have been responding to what political economists of the day *thought* was going on, rather than to a pervasive development in the real world.

Finally, and above all, the thesis does not sufficiently emphasise what may well have been the most important consideration for pre-industrial craftsmen – like the millwright or the hand-loom weaver – fighting for the status of a way of life: that is, *retaining control at the point of production*. If we add a 'high discretion content' to the usual definition of skill as a combination of knowledge and dexterity, then we may have found one of the reasons why so many people were so keen to defend what were in today's terms unskilled occupations at the time of the Industrial Revolution. It was not necessarily a matter of protecting skills, as Morris thought, but rather of protecting the measure of control the craftspeople exercised over their work – in their own time, to their own pace, perhaps with their own machinery. No one can ever agree about what the components of 'skill' are because clearly all skills are different. If we extend the concept to *the circumstances which make possible any skilled activity*, we can find much use for the deskilling thesis in the present. For although today's various types of craftsmen may argue forever about the process itself (does skill involve mental or manual dexterity, or both?) they all seem to have a common, strong belief in the importance of controlling every aspect of the work they do, and having the *time* to control every aspect of the work they do. There is no need to bring nostalgia into the picture at all.

If we go further and relate this issue of *control* to the role of tomorrow's craftsmen in society, we can see why it is so crucial to abandon the other static notion of skill held by the Arts and Crafts people. For it will be possible in the near future for whole industries to be made up of small interconnected workshops, each in specialised areas, each allowing for a large measure of control at the point of production within each unit, together catering for a market which wants well-made and customised products rather than badly made identical ones. The centre for such production in the mid-1980s has been in 'the middle Italy'. Emilia, Romana, Tuscany, Umbria and the three Venetian provinces, a region which is sharply contrasted with, on the one hand, the industrial north of Italy – Milan, Turin and Genoa (where the cars are hand-built by robots) – and, on the other hand, the agricultural south where the traditional rural crafts still have important parts to play.

Here in 'the middle Italy', in small workshop-based activities, there are craft industries as diverse as shoes, ceramic tiles, textiles and furniture. In these a huge variety of craft goods is produced through the cooperation of networks of small firms each employing around ten craftsmen. The thing that has made this possible is the development of numerically controlled machine tools or robots – but robots harnessed to the ever-changing needs of small batch or short run production. These small interconnected firms have proved themselves relatively immune to economic crises of over-production at a time when large, inflexible, highly automated, deskilled firms are going to the wall. By any definition this success is related to skilled craftsmanship; so it may not be a question in the near future of 'industry versus craft' but of 'craft with industry', of a product hand-built with just a little assistance from robots. Industries of a few people, creating local networks with new kinds of tools, maybe linking with larger networks …

# 4. The Professor of Digging

IN THE AUTUMN of 1874, John Ruskin asked some of his Oxford students to help finish a project which he had begun the previous Spring – the building of a country road, complete with borders of flowers, to take the place of the existing swampy lane which ran past Ferry Hinksey. The students would rise at dawn, do a spot of digging and paving and then be rewarded with a hearty breakfast in Ruskin's wood-panelled rooms: the heavy work would take place under the expert guidance of David Downs, Ruskin's aged gardener and handyman whom the Slade Professor of Fine Art had originally invited to come to Oxford as the first 'Professor of Digging'. For Ruskin – who was simultaneously giving a series of eight packed-to-the-rafters lectures on 'The Aesthetic and Mathematic Schools of Art in Florence' – the exercise had many purposes, some solemn and some not-so-solemn: it was much more useful, as physical exertion and indeed as art, he said, than 'fruitless slashing of the river' and 'hitting a ball with a bat'; it might help to demonstrate his long-held view that manual work could itself be educational (as a training in the skills of observation, accuracy and physical control); it would give his young Humanities students some experience of the drudgery and 'self-contempt' of many manual occupations, which could perhaps lead to some changed attitudes; since he tended to lecture at some length on the moral value of human skills, even in the lowliest of occupations, from the Middle Ages onwards, the exercise might also function as a useful teaching aid; and maybe it would result in an attractive country road rather than the dirty and dingy lane which was little more than a path. Above all, the repairs at Ferry Hinksey would bring home to his young charges two great lessons about which Ruskin had quite recently written, in *Sesame and Lilies* and *Time and Tide:*

> We live, we gentlemen, on delicatest prey, after the manner of weasels; that is to say, we keep a certain number of clowns digging and ditching, and generally stupefied, in order that we, being fed gratis, may have all the thinking and feeling to our selves.
>
> Let a man once learn to take a straight shaving off a plank, or draw a fine curve without faltering, or lay a brick level in its mortar, and he has learned a multitude of other matters which no lips of man could teach him.

In today's far less elegant terminology, 'the division of mental and manual labour', and the importance of the 'tacit knowledge' of the craftsman: both of them at the centre, then as now, of the debate about craft skill in particular and the labour process in general. Ruskin was writing – and engaging in his eccentric educational experiment – at a time when the crafts, as distinct from the products of the manufactories, had become *visible* for the first time. And by becoming visible, they had also – by contrast with the norm – somehow become admirable. Before then, they weren't either visible or admirable – they were just the way things were made: since there were very few replicas around, people had had to make do with prototypes. In the 1860s and 1870s, though, the crafts began to be set against the deskilling tendencies of the mid-Victorian age (and the theories of political economy which underpinned these tendencies). And the great division of 'creative work' versus 'the rest' was the long-term result. Art was wonderful, craft was admirable – while most manual occupations were either alienating or anomic or both, in the words of the very latest social theorists. As an elderly don in a C.P. Snow novel once said, 'nine English traditions out of ten date from the latter part of the nineteenth century'. The modern crafts, and the values they are expected to embody, were no exception. The repairs at Ferry Hinksey could teach the students about 'the rest'.

The road-gang included (amongst assorted Balliol men) Arnold Toynbee, who became foreman answering to the Professor of Digging, and Oscar Wilde, who was to boast that he had been given permission to fill 'Mr Ruskin's especial wheelbarrow' and had been given tuition by the Slade Professor himself in the subtle art of actually wheeling it. It would, hoped Wilde, be rather like building a Gothic Cathedral: well, almost. The gang particularly enjoyed the thought that the fruit of their labours had become the 'in' place for Oxford undergraduates and their partners to visit on a December Sunday afternoon. But, alas, as Wilde's biographer Richard Ellmann observes, it was soon time for these latter-day medieval masons to go on their respective vacations: 'the work went on in November to the end of term, after which Ruskin was off to Venice, and Wilde could again rise late, as the road for its part sank slowly from sight.' Ruskin had to agree that, whether or not his loftier aims had been realised, it really was the worst country road in the three kingdoms.

As P.D. Anthony has written in *John Ruskin's Labour* (1983), 'Ruskin's admiration for the qualities he saw in physical work has been widely shared, particularly by those who are not called upon to do very much of it.' Shared, for example, by the philosopher and the educationalist who are leaning against a rail on the right-hand side of Ford Madox Brown's famous Pre-Raphaelite painting *Work*: in the original sketch, there was just one of them – and he was an artist – but Brown was persuaded by the purchaser of the picture, Mr Plint of Leeds, in November 1856, to paint in the philosopher and the educationalist 'to give more fully the idea of the head and the heart of the work of the mind'. The hand would be represented by the muscular (and presumably mindless) navvies digging a hole ready for the introduction of a new sewage system under Heath Street, Hampstead. Madox Brown watched the hole being successfully dug. But the real moral of the tale of Ferry Hinksey was that the road never did get rebuilt.

* * *

In the first manifesto of the Staatliches Bauhaus (1919), the so-called 'handicraft' manifesto, with its woodcut cover of the cathedral of the arts by Lyonel Feininger, Walter Gropius wrote one of the great catchphrases of modern art and craft education: 'Artists, architects, sculptors,' he declaimed, 'we must all return to the crafts.' Or so the British studies of the Bauhaus say. An end to Salon art and art for art's sake! An end to the art which has no living link with the realities of matter, technique, economy! The beginning of the unity of all creative arts within the new architecture! The foundation of the great building! It is a catchphrase which has – since that time – often been set in opposition to Marcel Duchamp's equally famous line, 'it's art if I say it's art' (a line, incidentally, from which Tom Stoppard has recently derived much comic mileage). After all, Gropius's manifesto seems to anchor art practice in a 'return to the crafts' – and is thus the great polemical antidote to all those readymades, conceptual extravaganzas, found objects and examples of 'imagination without skill' which have overflowed from Duchamp's urinal, or 'Fountain', signed R. Mutt, ever since 1917.

Or is it?

Actually, the phrase 'we must all return to the crafts' – which has fitted like a nice, woolly teacosy over much Anglo-Saxon thinking about the crafts and tradition – is a mistranslation. What Gropius really wrote was 'we must all turn to the crafts':

meaning the contemporary crafts, and especially those up-to-date ones which, he hoped, would be available in the local region. Not a return, or a U-turn, but a straightforward 'turn'. It was, as Gropius later added, a question of the crafts shedding their 'traditional nature' and becoming instead 'research work for industrial production, speculative experiments in laboratory-workshops where the preparatory work of evolving and perfecting new type-forms will be done'. This was the 'turn' which so impressed Herbert Read in *Art and Industry*. And yet almost every British book about the Bauhaus still prefers to interpret the manifesto as a plea for the skills of yesterday, to help artists find their way through the visual complexities of the today: after all, didn't Gropius write that he was 'determined to transfer into practice' the ideas of his mentors John Ruskin and William Morris?

It has also proved comforting to commentators and educationalists alike to imagine that everyone involved in the project agreed with what Gropius had to say. After all, this was the golden – or should that be tubular steel? – age, the 'ideal' (in Nikolaus Pevsner's words) 'of a twentieth century art school. An extraordinarily brilliant staff of architects, craftsmen and artists, representing the most advanced tendencies in art as well as the soundest principles...'

Again, this is a mythtranslation. As is the thought that Gropius's clarion-call had the monopoly on advanced thinking. In 1922, the design educator Adolf Behne published an essay called *Art, Handicraft, Technology*, which – in no uncertain terms – attempted to take apart Gropius's assumptions about craftsmanship (even modern craftsmanship) and creative skill. 'Artists, architects, sculptors,' he wrote, 'must we all return to handicraft, must we all turn to the crafts? No, we must not. We must proceed – to the service of spirit and imagination and intellect!' Behne's full-blooded remarks, which begin with the assumption that the debate is really about society's 'own attitude towards its own work methods', are well worth excavating as much-needed nourishment for the debate of today:

> If one speaks of craftsmanship [writes Behne] one implies praise. If one speaks of technique, on the other hand, one implies criticism, or at least reservation and doubt.
>
> The notion is that craftsmanship is something inspired, technique something superficial and mechanical.
>
> The notion has become widespread and is responsible for many false conclusions.
>
> Craftsmanship has become a catchword. In the preference for craftsmanship, a sentimental romanticism is revived one last time before the consciousness of the times decisively turns away from the old order. Society's view of the relationship of the artist to his material accurately reflects its own attitude toward its own work methods. The resolve to usher in the new order from its modest, fragile beginnings through

conscious endeavour is so difficult that a last attempt is made to take refuge in the (presumably!) beautiful, good and simple past. Only when this attempt has proved hopeless will the task of the times be recognised and dealt with…

Can one really dispute the fact that there are innumerable handcrafted products which are loveless, indifferent, banal and superficial? Is there not also mechanical work in handiwork, and can one maintain that work aided by technology cannot be exceptionally inspired and conscientious?

The breaking of the natural unity in which the inventor is simultaneously the executor can open the way to a higher intellectual-artistic perfection…

At one level, it's Behne's aggressive modernism versus Gropius's mystical manifesto: one with his eye on the road ahead, the other looking in the rear-view mirror and at the road ahead, both at the same time. But, at another, the essay is remarkable for the way it points towards more recent analyses of skill and craftsmanship. Skills are not necessarily 'lost', argues Behne; rather they are redistributed in new ways and through new forms. The assumption that pre-industrial skills were always part of a 'beautiful, good and simple past,' he continues – that they were highly skilled, in today's terms – may well be too sentimental. As Gordon Russell once wrote of Ford Madox Brown's sunlit image of *Work* – it implanted in the mind a 'tidied-up, suburban, Pre-Raphaelite variety of navvy'. The concept of 'craft', the essay goes on, is usually contrasted with something called 'industry' (or 'technique'), when in fact the two developed side by side, in many areas, throughout the nineteenth century, and there are still many possible models of connection between the two. Above all, Behne concludes, it is not a question of skilled individuals versus unskilled teams – but of a new-style division of labour, one based upon 'spirit and imagination', where each contributor is able to exercise a high level of discretion over his or her work, in a common purpose. The point is not to sit around telling sad stories, or to see the development of society – and 'its work methods' – as always a fall from grace, a decline from the good old days when relationships were still organic rather than mechanistic, but rather to recognise 'the task of the times' – and try to deal with it. The real moral of the tale is that the Bauhaus – despite all its rhetoric about the uniting of the arts with industry, and within building – remained at its heart an arts and crafts school: indeed by all accounts it was the monastic aspects of life there which, educationally, seemed to work best. Gropius understood the 'turn to the crafts' in theory, but in practice... he resigned from the School over this very issue of the crafts and batch or mass production.

# 5. Things Men Have Made

T HIS PUBLIC DIALOGUE on 'workmanship' and 'craftsmanship' with the craftsman in wood, teacher and writer David
Pye, was mainly about the issues raised in his classic book *The
Nature and Art of Workmanship* (1968). David had stressed that
he saw no point in 'going through the arguments and definitions in his books all over again': he preferred to discuss matters
which had arisen since *Workmanship* was first published, and
since his *The Nature and Aesthetics of Design* was issued in 1978.
And to take some well-aimed shots at the 'flock of duck-billed
platitudes' which tended in his view to surround contemporary thinking about craftsmanship. These matters included:
the aspiration of some crafts towards 'fine art', changing attitudes towards the canons of workmanship, the exhibiting of
the crafts, 'tacit knowledge' and the learning of craft skills, the
gospel according to St John Ruskin, the relationship between
workmanship and design, and the implications for the crafts of
digital technology.

Frayling: The first question is about developments within the
crafts since *The Nature and Art of Workmanship* was published.
You suggest that the crafts occupy a border ground between
Fine Art and Manufacture. Since the book was published, the
crafts – at least the more highly publicised examples – seem to

have aspired more and more to the condition of the Fine Arts, sometimes to the neglect of traditional standards of workmanship. Could you comment on the reasons for this development and its likely effects?

Pye: Well, I think the first thing to say about that is that really these categories, Fine Art and Craft and Manufacture and so on, are fairly meaningless. I think it's an old saying that all Art is one, but no one has ever been able to draw a line, cut-and-dried and hard-and-fast between Fine Art and Applied Art; between Fine Art and Craft; between Craft and Design – any of these things. And in this discussion I would like to say that when I say 'workman' or I suppose 'craftsman', I mean a man or a woman who simply makes things by the workmanship of risk – nothing else. I think one can quite usefully talk about a designer-craftsman, meaning a craftsman who designs what he makes, as opposed simply to a craftsman who has no hand in the design, but simply interprets somebody else's: for instance, a toolmaker, a pattern-maker. I'd also say that design is essentially an abstract and non-figurative art, and so of course is much Sculpture. And I should say, myself, that the criterion of Fine Art – the essential one – is that it is absolutely useless. It may be highly valuable, but it's quite, quite useless. That's the American Customs and Excise definition of Fine Art, and a jolly good one. It's meant for contemplation – it's not meant for use.

Well, having said that, I think that to make something which is for use imposes limits on the designer's freedom of choice –

94

it's no good designing chairs which can't be sat on because they come to pieces, and so on. And there are far more exacting limits than that. In fact, as a matter of observation, of people working on a design, the limits on one's freedom of choice in fact help the thing and don't hinder it – why that is exactly, I don't know. If you've got, as they say, 'a peg to hang your hat on' as a starting point, it simplifies the whole process.

And when you start producing abstract sculpture – as I've done in my time, God help me – the thing is infinitely more difficult: everything is possible, nothing can be ruled out of court. And there's something in here which keeps on saying, 'Well, that's no good, it's got to be more like this, it's got to be more like that.' And all of that is probably true, but when you have spent most of your life designing things, it really puts you into a cold sweat. So I think the fact that what they call 'the crafts' are edging rapidly, as far as I can see, in the direction of abstract art, is meaning that the process of producing them is getting much more difficult, and I think you can very, very often – regrettably often – see that. I think there's a great deal of stuff which is turned out which is terribly meretricious – it looks thin, it is thin. I think the famous saying of William Lethaby is very applicable to it – 'No art that is only one-man-deep can be very much good' – and a lot of it is, very obviously, only one-man-deep. It's highly original: well, originality – just originality and nothing else – is terribly easy to achieve. Anybody whatever can produce an original design, but, by God, what you want to do is to produce good design, and generally speaking the ingredients of good art are rather like the old Hallowe'en charm – 'something new, something old, something else…' Well, something new and something old are ingredients in any effective work of art. The point of the 'something old' is that tradition means anything but the common acceptance of it now; the one thing it doesn't mean is copying what's been done before. What it does mean is standing on the shoulders of what's been done before, starting with where what's been done before left off.

Frayling: Another thing that lies behind the recent debate about 'craft', 'art' and 'originality' is that in terms of your analysis of what's involved in workmanship – where there's a strong premium on what I used to call 'skill', but now tend to call 'dexterity, judgement and care' – a lot of this work is very shoddy in terms of precisely those values, although it may not be shoddy in terms of another set of values, a different kind of statement. The danger, of course, is that in the public mind the concept of 'craft' becomes associated no longer with those canons of workmanship, but with second-rate modernism. Now, that's the danger, I would have thought, from your point of view…

Pye: I think that, probably, is true.

Question from the floor: One of the problems with crafts – contemporary crafts – is that many people get involved in it because it is one of the few options that they have for exploring their potential: that the fast-moving industrial framework that we have a) cannot cope with such people and is not a broad-minded enough employer, b) is not particularly concerned with the sorts of values that we are generally concerned with – aesthetic values, taking care, doing things properly, being very good at something. So on the rebound, there is too much emphasis upon virtuoso craftsmanship for the sake of it – and for the sake of justifying the price. Actually, some of the most interesting work in the crafts seems to me to come closer to the design-making end of things.

Pye: I myself would like to see much more of people like instrument-makers for one thing, and much more of toolmakers and pattern-makers, shoemakers and all the rest of it. The workmanship of risk at its best, in fact, in any particular trade is what I would like to see.

Question from the floor: If you have a high-level gallery and they put on exhibitions and you take a pine stool and you put it on top of a white plinth, the impetus to actually add a bicycle wheel on top is almost unavoidable and you actually get a Duchamp-style object. The whole difficulty of showing design and craft in what is 'a gallery environment' by that action tends to elevate it – tends to move it in the direction of it being a work of art. Now, you take an ordinary wooden bench and put it on a plinth and you ask yourself, 'Is it Art or is it Craft?' – it becomes Art by the fact that you've put it on a plinth. A lot of things that don't look good in exhibitions would be perfectly acceptable at home. It's part of the dilemma, you see, that if you actually aspire to making things that other people would like to use, if you actually put that in an exhibition, it very often looks mundane. Because I don't ask of something I use that it should hit me in the eye every time I look at it. I don't want that out of a milk jug – I just want it to sit there docilely and contain the milk. If you put my milk jug in an exhibition, it just looks very ordinary. It doesn't have the sort of aura that an exhibition object is supposed to have.

Pye: We'd better forget the aura altogether – what I want to see is more milk jugs.

Frayling: There's general support for that! Let's move on now to the question of education and what is learned when you're learning a craft as distinct from what is learned when you're taught to design; a question that is stimulated by a quote from the design theorist, Philip Steadman in his recent book called *The Evolution of Design*.

It goes like this:

> In the craft tradition, since there are no radical departures from the repeated type, it is possible for artefacts to be made which are technically very sophisticated, which exploit physical principles, chemical processes or the properties of materials in very subtle ways but without any of their makers having a theoretical understanding of how these effects are achieved. The principles have been discovered empirically and are embodied in the inherited design. We might speak in a

sense of information being conveyed within the forms of the artefacts themselves. The craftsman knows how to make the object, he follows the traditional procedure, but in most respects he literally does not know what he is doing.

In other words, because the craftsperson doesn't necessarily understand the physical principles of the materials he's working, and because the techniques he is using have been discovered or experienced by doing, and because he can't write the project up like a scientist writes up an experiment – because of all these things the craftsman 'does not know what he is doing'. And the question is about the two kinds of knowledge that seem to me to be implied by the quotation. We have one kind of knowledge, the formal knowledge that Philip Steadman is talking about, about the principles of materials, materials science – things that you can write down in books and learn through the transmission of hard information. And we have another kind of knowledge, the tacit knowledge that you learn by doing, of experiencing things. This quotation suggests that what the craftsman experiences isn't knowledge at all, because it doesn't look like 'bits of information'. You can't express it in those terms and therefore it doesn't count as knowledge.

So the question is: in your book on *Workmanship* you follow a similar observation about craftsmen not necessarily understanding the physical properties of their materials, but with a very different conclusion: 'The truth is that what we want to do is not to express the properties of materials but to express their qualities.' Could you comment on the kind of knowledge which is embodied in the qualities of workmanship…?

PYE: To call it a kind of knowledge is a bit tricky, but still, I think the essence of the answer to that question is that I contend – and I'm not by any means the only one – a designer is a problem-solver: designing is essentially a problem-solving process. It is both essentially a problem-solving process and an art; it isn't one or the other – there's no one or the other about it; it's not 'either/or', it's 'both/and'. Well now, a designer or a craftsman, or what you like qua artist, most certainly doesn't know what he's doing: no artist has ever known what he's doing, as far as I can make out. No one has ever supposed that you can teach art – at least no one in their right mind has ever supposed you can teach art. But you can teach artists; and that is what this place is for – it's the Royal College of Art, it isn't the Royal College of something else. And if design should be proved – how, I've no idea – to be a problem-solving activity full stop, well then, let's close this place down jolly quick.

Now, there's not the slightest reason why efficiency and art should coincide: there's not the slightest reason why making a ship, which is a very good and useful ship, should also produce a beautiful ship. The funny nonsense that was called 'functionalism' which induced me to write the first part of that book 25 years ago maintained that it did. It maintained that things looked like that because they had to look like that, and so on;

whereas, as we all know, anyone who has practised design, a designer always has freedom of choice about the appearance of what he designs. And when I say 'always' I mean 'always'. I don't think I've ever come across an instance where he hadn't. I don't mean to say he has wide freedom of choice; he may have a very narrow freedom of choice, but that narrow freedom of choice may be crucial, absolutely. All that, I think, is part of the answer to this question... One wants to remember that there is a type of mind which is afraid of the mysterious, the non-rational, the apparently inexplicable, and that of course is art. Nobody has ever said, or been able to indicate, what art is essentially. So that it's impossible to deny what this chap says – that the artist or artisan doesn't know what he's doing – but that's not really a criticism of the artist at all. What exactly can one teach when one's teaching artists? Well, the first essential of teaching art is that the teacher must be an artist himself, otherwise the whole thing is pointless. The main thing, I think, is – the main thing that can be taught, I think, is, in a sense, not teaching at all – to give the chap a chance to find out what he can really do.

Question from the floor: One of the first great indictments – apart from the contemporary ones – of the Arts and Crafts Movement was in the writings of the economist, Thorstein Veblen, who said that all this stress on the roughness and on the things that were improvised was a sign of conspicuous consumption because they could then cost a lot more than everything else: if you had something which didn't look 'right' you knew that it was handcrafted and therefore was expensive, but if you had something that looked absolutely perfect it was machine-made and didn't cost so much. So it's all part of the aristocratic conspicuous consumption syndrome – the whole ambiguity on which the Arts and Crafts Movement is based

Pye: I should have thought that was absolute rubbish, wouldn't you? I mean, if ever there were really high-minded people it was the early people in the Arts and Crafts Movement, and I can't believe that they even knew what conspicuous consumption was! I mean, they went about with their heads in the clouds, eating grass, as far as I can make out!

Frayling: The reason this is so relevant today is that a small group of critics – such as Peter Fuller – is trying hard to put the 'ethics' back into 'aesthetics'. The critique of Modernism and the Avant-garde is getting to the stage where some art critics are saying, 'Bring the ethics back and bring them back through a revised version of what John Ruskin and William Morris were saying.'

Pye: There's another thing that might well be said before we get going on that: the thing which Morris, more or less quoting Ruskin, said was that it was wicked to make man do tedious, repetitive work, and that unless there was joy in the labour nothing could be said for it. Well, some people like tedious, repetitive work; everybody, I think, likes a bit of it now and then; and when you get to my age there isn't a hell of a lot of joy in labour, believe me! It gets you round here! And that really is a point because, you see, in those days people aged a lot quicker than they do now, and by the time you were forty and over you weren't going to enjoy labour an awful lot whatever kind it was.

Question from the floor: At one stage William Morris does say of the craftspeople in his workshops that he feels a kind of guilt towards them. They were, he thinks, happy enough in their work, but he says he is, in fact, deskilling them for work outside his workshops in the late nineteenth century; and if he went bankrupt all his workmen, who had learned all these skills, would be unemployable. So that was one of the reasons that he said he had to keep going even when making a loss, because he had responsibilities towards this little group.

Pye: That's interesting: I didn't know that.

Frayling: Which brings up the question about craft and design. In *The Nature and Art of Workmanship* you define the intended design as 'an ideal form to which the workmanship of risk may approximate'. Does this intended design need to be expressed before craftspeople start working or can it, does it in your view, emerge from the process of workmanship itself?

Pye: I think it certainly does want to be expressed before the chap starts working: it may be expressed only in his head, but he's got to have a clear idea of what he's going to do before he starts – a clear idea, but it may not be a very detailed idea. I don't think a design ever emerges as you go on working – it evolves. I mean that the skeleton of it, the basis of it, is there already, but when you start making, in three dimensions, something which is only dreamed up in here or shown in a sketch on a piece of paper, or even in a detailed drawing on a piece of paper, you see things which you hadn't allowed for and you therefore modify the design accordingly. But you must at every stage in making something have a clear idea of what you're trying to do, even if you keep on changing the point of attack slightly as you go on – you must have a clear idea of why you're doing it. And that's a very old one. The whole thing, you see, turns on the ability to visualise things which aren't there – and that, I think, varies in different people. I believe it could be taught – I've no idea how – but I do believe it probably can be taught.

Frayling: In the book, you talk about 'the formalising of design' – in other words, the drawings – and the relationship between the drawings and the making of things. And you suggest these are wholly separate processes, although the latter can enhance the former – you tend to separate the two.

Pye: But the drawing is only expressing the ideal form of what's in the head, and when it's actualised by someone making from it, he's producing only an approximation to it – inevitably. But the basis of the whole thing is the thing visualised before it's drawn. That runs on to the next question, I think: can you be a good designer if you're not a good maker? Well, undoubtedly the answer is yes, you can: one has known people who could – Kaare Klint, who was perhaps the greatest furniture-designer of this century, so far anyway: I don't think he ever made anything, but all the Danish designers and cabinet-makers used to say about him, 'Klint has never made anything, but we all go and ask him how to do it!' Because he knew: he knew it absolutely backwards. Moreover, although he didn't have, apparently, a very acute ability to visualise the effect of what he was designing, he did know his own limitations and he would design a piece of furniture and have a model made of it – quarter full size or one-fifth full size – put it on the mantelpiece and look at it for a year before he put it into production, so as to really make up his mind whether he'd done as much towards it as he could.

Frayling: It's surprising you should say that about designing and making, because there are points in your book when you imply that you can only really be a good designer if you can fully understand the possibilities of the materials you're dealing with: which seems to me to be – to take it one step further – a sort of understanding that can only emerge if you have experience of working with the material.

Pye: No, I don't believe it is; I don't think so. I don't say that people who can do the thing are common – I shouldn't think they are at all, but they do exist. Dick Russell, who was the first Professor of Furniture at the Royal College of Art, he was pretty near as good as Klint. But there is one thing to be said about it: both Klint and Dick Russell designed nearly always with the same makers, throughout their lives – Kaare Klint worked with Rudolf Rasmussen and Dick Russell with the makers at Gordon Russell Ltd. And when you work with a maker as closely as that, and you know each other as well as that, the thing becomes much more manageable. I can remember on some occasion some-body – I suppose it must have been the Rector Robin Darwin – wanted something made for the Royal College of Art by last Thursday, and I designed it on a bit of squared paper in the train coming up to London, and I chucked it at Ron Lenthall, the cabinet-maker who worked for the Furniture Department, and said: 'Look, for God's sake get on with making that, because it's wanted by last Thursday, and when you find a snag come and tell me!' And he got on with it, and then he came and said, 'Well, look, this won't work,' and so we evolved another way of doing it; and then that wouldn't work, and so we evolved another way of doing it, and put the thing together and it was a passable job. Well, that would have been absolutely impossible if one was going to a cabinet-maker whom one had never seen before or didn't know anything about. So perhaps that's a quali-fication that should have been made, but I'm perfectly certain that it is possible to be a very good designer and not be a maker.

Frayling: It would put architects in an unusual position, otherwise.

Pye: Yes, it would – it would indeed.

Frayling: But does your attitude to the work change if you're creating something yourself?

Pye: No, not to the work itself, no, I don't think it does. And also, of course, the other fascination of working to some-body else's design is that you learn from it. I mean, I've once or twice worked at things that were designed by Professor Robert

Goodden (a trained architect who became a silversmith), and he was a jolly good designer. And I started off thinking, 'I wonder what the hell he's getting at with this?' And as I went on following it I saw the point. I don't think one's attitude to the actual work – that is to say, to the process of making what's there – is any different, but the amount of tension that goes with it is quite, quite different, I think.

Frayling: The final question arises out of a talk that somebody gave to a group of craftspeople here a while ago, concerning numerically-controlled or digital technology. A piece of wood carving was handed round the audience, and everyone said: 'Oh, the workmanship of risk – wonderful – it breathes all the vitality of handwork.' And then the lecturer said: 'Well, actually that was the result of a computer programme, of automation; a piece of robotic technology had been programmed to reproduce that piece an infinite number of times, to copy the movements of the hand,' at which point some people in the audience then said: 'Ugh – I don't like it any more.' Now, clearly your 'proof of the pudding is in the eating' philosophy – if I can put it that way – raises this question, because the work itself couldn't tell you anything about the process because it in fact had been programmed by an extremely skilful craftsman who was able to make it reproduce the finest detail of the prototype. With variations each time. So would it worry you?

Pye: No, not a bit. The computer's only a tool like any other tool and, if it'll do that, then jolly good luck to it. No, it doesn't bother me; it's the results I want – I don't care how you get them – it doesn't matter how you get them. But I'd be fascinated to see the sort of things I make turned out by a computer – I really would – I'd love to see it. I bet I could do it better than the computer, all the same!

Frayling: I'd like to finish with a quotation from a D.H. Lawrence poem – one which Edward Barnsley and the Cotswold craftspeople used often to cite. In fact, Edward quoted it in his very last lecture. It's called *Things Men Have Made*. I'm sure you know it, David, and I hope you feel it is appropriate:

> Things men have made with wakened hands,
> and put soft life into are awake through years with
> transferred touch,
> and go on glowing for long years.
> And for this reason, some old things are lovely
> warm still with the life of forgotten men who made
> them.

# 6. The Medium and the Message

THE TRANSFER OF images created by fine artists from one medium, or even one dimension, to another, is so much part of everyday life that we all take the process for granted. An oil painting becomes a chocolate box. A Victorian genre scene becomes a waxwork, or a hologram. A gallery-full of Giacometti figure sculptures suddenly turns into a puppet show, to advertise a bank on television. A Mondrian turns into a rock video. Dr Caligari's cabinet becomes serious interior design. A Henry Moore drawing is carefully worked into a tapestry. A scene from a film becomes a *tableau* which reminds us of a famous painting – always, by definition, a famous one. Images which are still part of the *Shock of the New* are used to help us recognise a brand of cigarettes. The process was predicted by Walter Benjamin, some thirty years ago, in *The Work of Art in the Age of Mechanical Reproduction*. He thought that the 'aura' of the original work of art would be withered by it, and that viewers would in future look at a work of art through the prism of its reproductions. Today, when both the art world and the mass media which feed off the images created by that world are part of a 'culture of quotations', things are not quite so clear cut. The lines are not so easy to draw. But we can still reassure ourselves that the fine artist *means* it, while everyone else is being ironic about it –

unless, of course, the fine artist was intending to be ironic in the first place. It's the artist as ecologist almost...

Nevertheless, when an *artist* moves from one medium, or one dimension, to another, we experience a different kind of unease – particularly in Britain. Partly, this is because there is still a hierarchy of art activities – fine art, applied art, decorative art, commercial art, or, to look at it the other way round, craft, designer-craft, artist-craft, fine art – and partly, this is because certain media are associated with one world (canvas, paper and oil = fine art), while other media belong further down the scale (wood, clay, fibre and elbow-grease = craft). A legacy of the Arts and Crafts people's obsession with natural materials, is that these still seem to occupy a higher place on the scale than the synthetic ones (plastic and polythene = industry). Of course, there have been craftspeople who have made very interesting use of synthetic materials (sometimes, as a gesture), and if you are a genius such as Picasso you can get away with anything. But there is still that unease. At a time when Julian Schnabel is incorporating ceramic plates and antlers into his work (how's *that* for the *Monarch of the Glen*?), and Anselm Kiefer is using bits of material culture such as reproduced images, lumps of lead and even a set of blacksmith's tongs to create layers of mythology, the unease is beginning to look very out of time. Did Julian Schnabel *make* those plates? And who cares? A lot of people, it seems.

Two years after Walter Benjamin wrote his essay, the philosopher R.G. Collingwood attempted to define the boundaries between 'what I shall call craft' and 'art proper' – from the point of view of the artist – in *The Principles of Art*. Writing in the wake of T.S. Eliot's *The Waste Land*, Collingwood stated that there was a prevailing misconception which encouraged 'people who write about art today to think that it is some kind of craft: this is the main error against which modern aesthetic theory must fight'. It was a misconception which he labelled 'the technical theory of art' – a theory which implied that art activity has something to do with 'the power to produce a preconceived result by means of consciously controlled action', and it only succeeded in confusing 'what I shall call craft' with 'art proper'; 'a technician is made', he could confidently add, 'but an artist is born'. If a 'theory of art' continued to lay so much stress on *mere* craft technique, Collingwood concluded, 'it is no more to be called art criticism, or aesthetic theory, than the annual strictures in *The Tailor and Cutter* on the ways in which Academy portrait painters represent coats and trousers'. The words 'artist' and 'artisan' may have the same linguistic origins, but that is where all similarity ended. It was as simple as that. But people *still* had the sneaky feeling that *The Waste Land* wasn't really poetry...

More recently, the American sociologist of art Howard Becker has studied what happens when members of 'the art world' begin to invade 'the craft world', and when 'the craft world' itself develops a concept of the *avant-garde* for the first time. What happens, in American colleges, studios and journals, is that the 'commonsense folk definitions' of these two activities have to be radically rethought. Normally, Becker suggests, we can rely on the folk definitions to tell us what 'art' and 'craft' actually involve: according to these definitions, members of the craft world possess a body of knowledge and skill which can be used to produce useful objects, and they have the ability to perform in a way which meets someone else's practical needs; members of the art world, by contrast, have no interest in the conventional standards of practical utility, they downgrade 'the old craft standards of skill', and their work is done 'in response to problems intrinsic to the development of the art and freely chosen by the artist'. These folk definitions are only seriously called into question when the two activities, craft and art, are undergoing social change, for example when concerns 'characteristic of the folk definition of art' (aesthetic standards) begin to merge with concerns 'characteristic of the folk definition of craft' (standards of utility and skill). Such a 'typical historical sequence' – which occurred in America in the 1960s and in Britain in the 1970s – may eventually lead to a situation where craftsmen turn 'to the art world itself as a source of value', and begin to lay emphasis on 'the relative freedom of the artist from outside interference with his work'. Once this has happened, 'the organisational form of the craft world becomes more complicated than it might otherwise be', involving two distinct groups of people, opening up 'new organisational settings in which to work and gain support for one's work', and encouraging kinship between craftspeople and fine art institutions. All this is reflected in publications and institutions, exhibitions and shows, which are exclusively associated with one group or the other. Becker's conclusion is that the same activity, using the same materials and skills in what appear to be similar ways, may be called by either title, as may the people who engage in it; the activity may *look* the same from the outside, but the organisational setting has changed, as has the emphasis on concerns 'characteristic of the folk definition of art', and this has led to a new image and status. Matching this social movement of some craftspeople into the art world, there is a parallel movement the other way round as 'some artists look for new media in which to explore a current expressive problem'. This new breed of artists produces standards that are 'aggressively non-utilitarian' and the organisation of their work remains within the art world proper. 'It becomes a virtue not to display conventional craft virtuosity, and the artist may deliberately create crudities either for their shock value, or to show that he is free of that particular set of conventional restraints.' At this stage, the artist may well be in a position to present him or herself as 'a heroic individualist' – for 'artists working in conventional craft media are relatively freer than artist-craftsmen who work in the same media; for example, in the diversity of objects they can make'. And the previous generation of craftspeople is likely to become enraged at this invasion of their world. When these twin processes happen – craftsman enters the art world, while artist hijacks craft – 'for most of the people involved, the experience is much more one of choice among alternative institutional arrangements and working companions than of creative expressive leaps'.

The technical language of Becker's analysis may come as something of a shock; it is unusual, even today, for writers on art to use phrases such as 'organisational form'. But his point is a useful one. If, for Collingwood, the problem was about philosophy, for Becker the problem is about sociology – about the artist's or the craftsman's choice of working companions, and the organisations to which they belong. In neither case has the *medium* of expression got much to do with it.

Becker was writing at a time when the 'action-crafts' of 1950s America (which had abandoned the traditional values of good practice, to emphasise craft as abstract art) and the 'funk-crafts' of 1960s West Coast America (which had been allied to the Pop Art movement, with a shared interest in the imagery of mass culture) had introduced a concept of an *avant-garde* into the crafts for the first time, and as a result had decisively blurred the boundaries between the 'fine artist' and the 'craftsman'. The artists such as Peter Voulkos and Robert Arneson who moved into the craft world in the 1950s and the 1960s seemed to be free from (or blissfully ignorant of) the holy writ among craftspeople which said 'there is no beauty without utility'. The West Coast craftspeople who moved into the art world at the same time, with their ceramic Mickey Mouses and their funky versions of everyday objects, were probably aware of William Morris and the Arts and Crafts (or rather, of a hippie version which made the strange connection between Morris and Zen Buddhism), but they weren't going to allow *that* to restrict the aesthetic possibilities which were open to them. And in any case, it wasn't their tradition. The commonsense folk definitions of 'craft' (as virtuoso skill) and 'art' (as self-expression) were beginning to distract from the appreciation of modern work – such as the sculptural furniture of Wendell Castle. The *Objects USA* which resulted from this radical redefinition were immediately, and predictably, dismissed by the English potter Michael Cardew as 'Rubbish USA'.

By the 1970s, the phenomenon had reached British art schools – and was to travel, via the Crafts Council, to galleries and museums as well. When a selection of British craftspeople were asked by *Crafts* magazine, at the beginning of the 1980s, which books had influenced their thinking and work during the last ten years, amongst the many replies, the writings of John Ruskin, William Morris, C.R. Ashbee, George Sturt, Bernard Leach and David Pye were not mentioned once. Instead, the furniture designer and maker Fred Baier (whose reply was the first to be quoted) wrote: 'I'm not a great reader of books, especially not ones without pictures.... As far as books and work, the first one that springs to mind is Groucho Marx's *Letters*....

One book that did get to me was *The Principles of Art* by R.G.
Collingwood. I remember enjoying the Collingwood.'

Before the redefinition of the 1970s, the popular traditional
view of the crafts would have gone something like this:

- Crafts must be made of natural materials, preferably in
  beige;
- Crafts must be functional;
- Crafts must be the work of one person, perhaps featuring
  visible thumbprints or surface imperfections to prove it;
- Crafts must be the embodiment of a traditional design (unless
  of a musical instrument);
- Crafts must be in the 'artisan' rather than the 'fine art' tradi-
  tion;
- Crafts must be rural products;
- Crafts must be untouched by fashion (which, it went without
  saying, meant 'badly made fashion')
- Crafts must be easily understood;
- Crafts must last, like a brogue shoe or a fine tweed;
- Crafts must be affordable (even if, like William Morris's work,
  affordable mainly by Oxbridge colleges, Anglican churches
  and collectors);
- Above all, crafts must provide a *solace*, in a rapidly changing
  world.

After the redefinition, a fashionable, less traditional view of the
crafts would go something like this:

- Crafts can be made with machines and maybe even by them, if numerically-controlled technology goes on improving;
- Crafts can be made with synthetic materials, in all colours of the rainbow;
- Crafts can be non-functional, and may even conform to the American Customs definition of 'art' – that it must be totally useless;
- Crafts can be made in limited production;
- Crafts can be designed by one person and made by another (as they often were, in fact, in the original Arts and Crafts period);
- Crafts can provide designed prototypes for industry;
- Crafts can be made in towns, and usually are;
- Crafts can be high fashion, and *still* be well made, although they needn't be;
- Crafts can use ideas borrowed from the fine arts of painting and sculpture; they can even inhabit the *avant-garde*;
- Crafts can be transient;
- Crafts can be very expensive indeed (again, like most of William Morris's work; the late Victorians were prepared to pay for quality);
- Above all, crafts needn't provide a *solace* – their role is rather to provide a *challenge*, often by means of an ironic statement about traditional notions of 'the crafts'.

From being the only begetter of the 'artist-craftsman' or the 'fine art workman', William Morris had become, in the words of one design commentator in the late 1970s, 'that silly old bugger with muesli in his beard'. And the *avant-garde* craftspeople had come to resent *deeply* the traditional view, which is, of course, still the most widespread view in contemporary Britain. In his introduction to a key British exhibition of 1973, *The Craftsman's Art*, James Noel White wrote:

> Painting is becoming sculpture, is becoming ceramic, is becoming three-dimensional weaving, is becoming jewellery. Perhaps in our own *fin de siècle*, sculpture, not architecture, is the mother of the arts (as it probably was pre-historically) and the success of British sculptors in the Fifties and Sixties may have something to do with it…

Clearly, the 'commonsense folk definitions' are up for grabs. Not only where 'the craft world' is concerned, but where 'the art world' is concerned as well. It is only the outmoded hierarchies of the Victorians which prevent us from grasping the fact. The message from the medium, insofar as it is a 'message' at all, is that it ain't the way that you do it, it's what you do. But, even when this message has got through, most craftspeople (or, come to that, most artists) today would surely agree with Tom Stoppard's Henry Carr, when he dared to take issue with the poet Tristan Tzara in the play *Travesties*:

I might claim to be able to fly … 'Lo,' I say, 'I am flying.' 'But you are not propelling yourself about while suspended in the air,' someone may point out. 'Ah no,' I reply, 'that is no longer considered the proper concern of people who can fly. In fact, it is frowned upon. Nowadays, a flyer never leaves the ground and wouldn't know how.' 'I see,' says my somewhat baffled interlocutor, 'so when you say you can *fly* you are using the word in a purely private sense.' 'I see I have made myself clear,' I say. 'Then,' says this chap in some relief, 'you cannot actually *fly* after all?' 'On the contrary,' I say, 'I have just told you that I can.' 'Don't you see you are simply asking me to accept that the word Art means whatever you wish it to mean; but I do not accept it…'

The last fifteen years have certainly been a confusing period in the history of the crafts, at many levels. There has been an atmosphere of 'work-in-progress' about them. And this has been reflected in the Polonius-like array of terms which have been chosen to describe the practitioners who have made their names since the early 1970s, sometimes because of 'craftsman' seeming gender-specific. As long ago as 1965, the World Crafts Council suggested a range of not-very-useful categories within the overall concept of 'the craftsman':

Artisan-craftsman – one who executes traditional designs or the designs of others;

Artist-craftsman or designer-craftsman – one who is capable of originating his own designs and who exhibits and sells them under his own name;

Designer in the craft field – one who knows the techniques in given media but prefers to design work for others rather than execute it himself.

Since then, the prefixes artist- and designer- have at one time or another been added to just about every activity in which craftsmen or craftspeople engage. On the west coast of America there are even artist-plumbers. In Britain, the basic categories appear to have been reduced to 'artist-craftsman', 'designer-craftsman' and 'journeyman-craftsman' (although David Pye still prefers the word 'workmanship' to 'craftsmanship'; many people resent the connotations of 'journeyman'; and there are fierce disputes about the relative merits of 'craftsman' and 'craftsperson' for obvious reasons.) Recently, there has been a revival of the nineteenth-century categories 'decorative artist' and 'applied artist', as a way of side-stepping the problem by entirely missing the point. It is ironic, and rather sad, that today's craft world may be in danger of ending up where it started – with the Victorian concept of the 'fine art workman', although he or she won't actually be called that.

# 7. Shape Shifting

THE SURPRISINGLY FLUID concept of 'the crafts' is on the move again. Product design, at the high end, has been overlapping for some time – hence the important recent exhibition *Industry of One*: this showed the work of a range of exciting post-Seventies product designers who had decided to manufacture their own work as one-offs or batches rather than exhaust themselves knock, knock, knocking on industry's door. The resulting pieces on display were often indistinguishable from the work of craftspeople who had approached their products in a very different frame of mind. Did this matter?

Art at the high end, though, isn't overlapping with the crafts – the most publicised of contemporary artists have very little in common with makers. They get people to make things for them; they are more interested in concept than in what the philosopher R.G. Collingwood called 'the technical theory of art'; they aim for big white gallery spaces rather than domestic interiors. At the dawn of neo-conceptualism in the mid-Seventies, the industrial designer Misha Black argued in his lecture *Craft: Art or Design?* (great title) that the crafts would increasingly occupy the space vacated by conceptual art – for those collectors and consumers who wanted something tangible to take home: the art tended to be about nihilism and disillusionment while 'craftsmanship is normally concerned with the making of objects for use, for adornment, for worship or for play … it is a reaffirmation of social value'. The lecture began with the story of three graduates in Fine Art from Leeds Polytechnic who had walked 150 miles in East Anglia with a ten-foot yellow pole attached to their heads. Black's article could easily be updated. But this occupation of the vacant space has not in fact occurred on any great scale.

Public subsidy, from the same pot of money as the arts though not as design, has not resulted in an equivalence of profile, esteem, attention or exposure for the crafts. For complex educational, social and economic reasons – including a strong element of snobbery in the mix, not all of it one way – the crafts are still restricted to their own galleries, magazines, critical vocabulary, social networks and criteria of quality, unless you happen to be called Hans Coper. The American sociologist Howard Becker contended that the difference between 'the art world' and 'the craft world' is purely sociological – a matter of social groupings and their preferred outlets. He may well be right. But that does not make social mobility any easier.

The gulf between the two social worlds *may* begin to narrow: after all, the urge to possess 'positional goods' – that is, goods which other people can't have – has driven the art economy for centuries. So the crafts may indeed begin to enter the empty fortress. It is more likely, though, that as pundits become bored with conceptual art – many already have – artists will move on, and another neo-ism will emerge. One which is as keen as ever to distance itself from the craft world and the 'technical theory of art'.

The crafts meanwhile will become increasingly confident about their place within contemporary interiors and the life-style pages of culture/style magazines. They will easily distance themselves from television makeover programmes. At the avant-garde end, they will continue to make more or less esoteric comments about the rest of the craft world. But the heartland of the crafts will lie with contemporary interiors – and the makers will work more and more closely in teams with interior design-ers, architects, product designers, computer interaction design-ers and installation people. They will be completely at home with the full implications of modernity.

But three things will have to happen first. The crafts in education – primary, secondary and tertiary – must be allowed to breathe, even though they tend to be expensive and space-consuming. 'Making' – taking time over making things – must be valued. The crafts establishment must let in younger people, new blood. Like many who had to fight hard for recognition, the crafts establishment, mainly from the Seventies generation, seems to be finding it difficult to let go. There must, finally, be a national museum of the crafts – and I mean a museum, with a collection, gallery, archives and seminar room attached – to exhibit, study and debate the various traditions of the crafts which have emerged over the last century and a quarter, since the arts and crafts pioneers, and to locate them within the best of contemporary practice. And to relate these traditions to the shifting practices and procedures of art and design.

# 8. The New Bauhaus

THE title of this essay involves an element of prediction which is always high risk in the unpredictable worlds of art and design. So let me start, as a cautionary tale and as a curtain-raiser, with the example of a designer who thought he was rather good at looking ahead. It is the example of one Thomas Midgley, a very clever American designer and chemist in the early decades of the twentieth century. In 1916 Thomas Midgley was researching the problem of 'knock' in the internal combustion engines of the earliest cars – and he found that he could suppress this knocking effect by adding iodine to petrol. Later research showed that the molecular structure of fuel determines whether it 'knocks' or not. A series of additives was tried, and some were rejected as unacceptable – one made exhaust gases smell of garlic! Eventually tetra-ethyl lead was found to be by far the most effective. It was tested and declared safe by the US Surgeon General, and its subsequent introduction contributed substantially to the rapid growth of comfortable automotive transport across the world as the first generation of cars gave way to the second. So it was Midgley who, with the very best intentions in the world, first introduced lead into petrol. It solved his immediate problem, but it had all sorts of unforeseen consequences.

Thomas Midgley next turned his attention to refrigerants. At the time toxic chemicals were in common use in refrigerants, and leaks could be very harmful. Our hero solved the problem by developing CFC gases, which appeared to be inert and non-toxic. We know better now, but at the time he thought that CFCs would actually protect the public from harmful poisons. So it was the same Midgley who, still with the best intentions in the world, first introduced CFCs into refrigerants and enabled the modern refrigerator to happen. To misquote Oscar Wilde, 'to be responsible for one environmental disaster could be called unfortunate, to be responsible for two is little short of carelessness'.

And then Thomas Midgley in later life became seriously disabled, and he invented for himself a hoist to help him get in and out of bed. When trying to use it one day, he hanged himself by mistake – literally hoist by his own petard. Even his death occurred with the very best of intentions. A real-life cautionary tale.

But, bearing all this in mind, and with the shade of Thomas Midgley hovering over us, I want to share some thoughts on the education of young artists, craftspeople and designers for the future.

First a flashback, to the turn of the twentieth century, and the 1901 end-of-course student exhibition at the Royal College of Art, which was in those days held in London's Victoria and Albert Museum. The designer and illustrator Walter Crane,

my predecessor as head of the College, had recently reorgan-
ised the curriculum, to face what *he* saw as the challenges of the
new twentieth century. What was happening in his College was
happening in a lot of others as well. The key, said Crane, was
to engage in a debate with the new world and organisation of
manufacturing industry, not by stimulating it but by criticising
it through the medium of beautiful one-off pieces or artefacts
within a craft tradition, which would be seen by the public as
criticisms of the general shoddiness of the mass-produced goods
available in the high street.

'One hour of creative life says "yes", he wrote, 'but all the
others say "no"... we are gradually impoverishing the soil while
we are forcing the crops.' It was crafts education against the
world, and the model of how the College studios were to be run
was the alternative one of the medieval workshop with 'masters'
and 'apprentices', rooting the crafts in a social organisation. In
fact, a book was soon to argue forcefully that art schools should
take over the old craft apprenticeships. It was called *Should
We Stop Teaching Art?* So the exhibition of 1901 was all about
calligraphy and lettering (not yet graphic design), embroidery
and weaving (not yet fashion), woodcarving (not yet furniture
design), stained glasswork (not yet glass and ceramics), model-
ling (not yet sculpture) and mural painting (not yet painting)
– all with a slight touch of the new art, Art Nouveau, about it.

That was the view from 1901: a reaction against the industrial system of the day. That was how an art, craft and design

education institution came to terms with industrial developments which were going on outside it. Outside the show, in Exhibition Road, SW7, were parked horse-drawn carriages and one or two of the new horseless carriages as well. They will never supersede the bicycle, said one optimistic bicycle manufacturer. Rather like the gentleman in the Foreign Office who, when asked if he supported the introduction of the new Bell telephones, famously replied 'Why? We have messenger boys enough!' Inside the show of 1901 the only reference to industry and its possibilities was a series of agnostic comments by Arts and Crafts writers, such as: 'We are here to further the advancement of art in its application to industry. Are we sure that we do not mean the advancement of industry by the application of art?' The new century, it seemed, would be about expensive hand-made objects which were intended as a criticism of what was seen as the poor quality of those in the high street. Moving Pictures, projected at precisely the same time in an amusement arcade down the road in Piccadilly, were an end-of-pier kind of entertainment and the feeling in the College was no doubt that they would probably never catch on. Staff and students had recently closed their annual show by performing *A floral fantasy in an English country garden* in Kensington Gardens. The story, written by Walter Crane, concerned the good fairy of the crafts putting to shame the demons of industry who were called Bogus and Philistinus.

Our exhibition of 1901 was certainly a step forward from the old Victorian system it had replaced, which had been cleverly satirised by Charles Dickens in the opening chapters of *Hard Times* and had consisted largely of reading grammars of ornament and copying plaster casts with a charcoal stick, day in day out, a system which one critic referred to as 'cast-rated'. The reaction is easy to mock now, but the curriculum of 1901 was in fact to have a profound influence on the Bauhaus, which operated in the two German towns of Weimar and Dessau, between 1919 and 1932. Walter Crane's celebrated slogan 'The true root and basis of all Art lies in the handicrafts' (from his *Arts and Crafts Essays* of 1903) became Walter Gropius's even more celebrated clarion-call of 1919, urging artists to 'turn to the crafts'. Crane and the British arts and crafts educators have never been given enough credit for this. Walter under the bridge ...

The Bauhaus was to become the most influential, as well as the most notorious, art school in the world during the first half of the twentieth century. Bauhaus, by the way, means 'bau'/ 'build', 'haus'/'place' or 'team'; therefore Bauhaus is 'the place where people build things'. It also echoes, deliberately, *Bauhütte,* meaning 'mason's lodge' which gives the word a slightly mystifying, medieval-ish ring. The Bauhaus curriculum, again trying to come to terms with the machine age and with the problem of educating a new kind of artist or designer who could flourish within a modern democratic society, emphasised specialised craft workshops, run by Masters and Technicians – again on the medieval, arts and crafts, model – where the students would either make one-off pieces or prototypes for industry, after studying for eight months the basic components of visual language: texture, colour, form, shape and materials. So you began by understanding the individual elements and how they might be conjugated and then you brought them together in the process of making or building, which helped you understand the tactile and sensual qualities of materials, just like Walter Crane's curriculum in London of twenty years before. W.R. Lethaby's basic design cause, pioneered within the arts and crafts curriculum, was another model for the Bauhaus equivalent.

The great debates at the Bauhaus were about the relative status of art and craft, and how the old hierarchy between them should go and how both art and design should turn to the crafts; about craft and industry – what was the relationship between prototype and manufacture; and about the role of spiritual values in a modern, increasingly materialist world. Some of the students wandered around Weimar in medieval tunics, with shaven heads, doing breathing exercises and looking for shops which sold vegetarian food, which caused something of a sensation in early 1920s, as you can well imagine. The Bauhaus even published a macrobiotic cookery book in 1926. A few products of the Bauhaus went into mass production: a table-lamp, a tubular steel chair, some metalwork, some textile designs. And these have become iconic objects of the twentieth century, reproduced in just about every picture book on design, and almost synonymous today with the Bauhaus as brand and the 'machine aesthetic' – the aesthetic of mid-1920s machines, that is. But many more products were made and finished by hand, as a criticism at various levels of the quality of most everyday things. And the iconic objects tended to be created by members of staff, or ex-students who had become members of staff – which is why most Bauhaus exhibitions today are about the staff of the School rather than the students, which is rather missing the point.

One big problem at the time was that the right kind of technology could not be accommodated in the workshops, and only a few local factories were prepared to play host to visiting staff and students, who looked and sometimes behaved like medieval mendicants. Another was that nearly all the workshop Masters were artists rather than designers, so they were much stronger on writing manifestos about industry and producing wonderful visual aids, especially Paul Klee's, than on practical results. Paul Klee's lecture notes were recently exhibited in the Hayward Gallery in London, in frames, as art pieces in their own right. The founder of the School, Walter Gropius, in fact resigned in 1928 over precisely this unsolved problem. He had been terrific at producing manifestos and pamphlets and curricula, with help from the artists on the staff, but the big dilemmas remained unsolved and in some cases un-addressed. During the School's fourteen years' existence, there were only about 1500 students in all, 150 at any one time, tiny by today's standards. It was a residential school, and some of the most memorable student experiences seem to have happened after the working day: elaborate parties, carnivals and theatre productions with larger-than-life costumes after the staff had gone home to their fashionably Modernist specially-designed apartments.

Yet, despite its small scale and its tendency to debate issues in abstract ways rather than always doing something about them, the Bauhaus was to have a huge influence on arts education in the industrial era: craft plus alternative philosophy, and the hope that industry might be listening; art meets design through making; the experimental workshop. It was to become itself a prototype. Not just in education but crucially in the design profession as well – with an emphasis on the importance of form, of *ideal* form, which has famously created difficulties for the profession in modern times. The architectural historian Nikolaus Pevsner wrote of the Bauhaus, 'For the first time in our century, there was an academy which was concerned with a genuinely contemporary expression of life: this was the lasting legacy of the Bauhaus.' Anni Albers, who was a student in 1922 and later became head of the weaving workshop, remembered it rather differently. She once admitted to me, 'The Bauhaus today is always seen as a coherent School, a very adventurous one, but a kind of ready-made. When I got there in 1922 that wasn't true at all. It was in a great muddle and there was a lot of searching going on. It was a series of ideas rather than a School.' Ideas, one could add, which set the agenda for the twentieth century, even if the old creativity and industry dilemma was left unresolved. Ideas which produced some fabulous manifestos, curricula and archives, however much or little they mapped onto reality. There was enough rhetoric for Gropius completely to redefine his contribution – minus the socialism – throughout the 1950s in America. But at least the School was discussing the dilemma, in a contemporary way. The Bauhaus did indeed produce some iconic objects. But the real research, on which industry depended, was of course happening elsewhere – in engineering, and materials science and chemicals and technology, and in the research and development sections of big businesses. Meanwhile, the Bauhaus was being translated into other educational experiments: Chicago in the 1940s, Dartington in the early 1950s, Ulm in the 1960s and so on.

Now, if one was founding a new Bauhaus – a new place where people build – for the early twenty-first century, and bearing in mind the caveat I mentioned at the beginning, what might *that* look like? A place where art, craft and design can engage with the post-industrial age, and with educating a new kind of artist or craftsman or designer or all three who in turn can flourish within a post-modern society and culture; a culture where we have moved on from net curtains to internet, from the space of places to the space of flows. Not learning grammars, or criticising products, but *engaging*, at a time when the very word 'products' is completely changing its meaning: 'sun products' for holidays; 'life products' for insurance; 'parking products' for leaving your car and even 'product design' for financial packages on the stock exchange! The Oxford English Dictionary still defines a product as 'a thing assembled or manufactured', but I guess that will soon change. In this world of flux, the staff and students of our new Bauhaus will by definition have a strong belief in the future, just as their forbears did in their manifestos and slogans. Not as any kind of feel-good factor, or in an uncontroversial or unchallenging way, but they will believe that doing something about it, and making a difference, is a worthwhile thing to attempt. They'll have their finger on the pulse of contemporary visual culture, they'll be flexibly-minded, multicultural (they will think of culture*s* rather than culture and they will come from culture*s* rather than culture), good at setting their own agendas and solving their own intellectual and visual problems, reflective thinkers through action, excited about using technology, highly motivated and full of attitude, completely at home in the digital universe, excited by an unpredictable world where the goalposts keep shifting and products are made of thin air, in tune with future market trends, and enterprising. They will indeed have a profound belief in the possibilities of the future.

'What's the point of the arts and crafts?', one of the founders of the Arts and Crafts movement, William Morris, was once asked just after he'd delivered a lecture on 'The Useful Arts' in Birmingham. His reply? The point of the arts, he replied, is to give us hope. Art and design students are already five times more likely to be self-employed than any other university graduates, and they are particularly good at constructing worlds around themselves in very entrepreneurial and improvisatory ways. Worlds where products and services seem to be blending together; where in-house has turned into in-system; where there's no longer a stable idea of function, something the original Bauhaus held dear; where design and craft are not just something you do *to* things, they are something that happens in a cultural and economic context; and where there's a sense of stimulating industry rather than criticising it or even serving it. Because the creative industries want above all to be stimulated with strong creative ideas. And the experimental workshop is a good place to start. So how might our new Bauhaus engage with the rapidly growing creative sector in the economy? And build bridges between the new economy and the old one?

Well, it will have three basic roles, whether it be freestanding or embedded in a big institution. It will be an *agency of professional education*, having close contact and two-way relationships with the professions of art, craft and design, through professional practitioners as teachers and examiners, as advisers creating an entrée into the networks or clusters the students will belong to when they leave; through being places to wire into, for mid-career professionals; through exploring the boundaries between research, development and advanced practice; through relationships with small and medium-sized businesses which understand and value educational and highly creative environments. Another firm link with these professional worlds will be our new Bauhaus as a cultural institution in its own right – with its exhibitions, its reaching out into the community in a much more generous and informative way than is usual at present, its space for sharing what it does and what it stands for – in the visual and the performing arts. Inside, for the first time ever, the technologies available to art, craft and design institutions will be much the same as those available to the professional worlds they will stimulate. Take rapid prototyping. On-screen information, provided by the craftsperson or designer, automatically models or cuts in resin or wax. This is transforming the design and making of objects. Instead of taking individual elements and assembling them through making – the Victorian grammars, the Arts and Crafts model and the Bauhaus basic course – the information on the screen embodies research, experience, and the understanding of materials. You still need intimate knowledge of materials, of course, but the tacit knowledge of the maker is beginning to *precede* the concept in some areas. The subsequent making of the prototype is becoming purely mechanical. The one-off crafts are again confronting the challenges of manufacturing. 'An industry of one.' In the fullness of time, that will become something to wire into, like the scientific laboratories of mainstream universities. But our new Bauhaus will not attempt to clone the professions; it will instead be what I call a 'radical academy', like the original one, and proud of admitting it. When people ask what work they do, artists and craftspeople will talk of their practice *and* of their professionalism as teachers and researchers in this setting. At the moment, if you ask artists who teach about what work they do, they never talk about their teaching. In our new radical academy, they will...

Allied to this, our new Bauhaus will also be *a research institute* for the creative industries, a key crucible for research and innovative applications within this burgeoning sector, performing a similar function to engineering and applied science within traditional universities in relation to manufacturing. A place of forward-looking practitioners. Not so much a think tank, as a 'think and do' tank, with the creative environment, the space, the expertise and the time to recharge batteries. Putting art next to craft next to design: art in a design environment, design in an art environment. After all, architects and installation artists, environmental artists and interior designers, painters and textile designers, sculptors and product designers, architects and craftspeople are moving closer to one another all the time. Innovative applications will include customising and humanising technologies; testing new materials, asking questions the consultants would never ask, making machines do things they were never meant to; asking what happens to objects when they've outlived their usefulness; bringing together the performing and visual arts. Research could include social applications such as inclusive design, design for everyone, design which really *understands* users, and a lifestyle laboratory or digital playground which businesses, artists and designers will want to wire into. And 'intelligent fabrics'. Maybe design against crime, as well. Design and risk. And what about research into 'emotional ergonomics'?

This *research institute* model places our new Bauhaus as not just part of the graduate supply chain but as a key part of knowledge interchange. As I've said, the creative industries want to be stimulated; they thrive on it. Our new Bauhaus will be an MIT for *design*. Not just for technology.

One paradox of this kind of action research in the early twenty-first century is bound to be that, on the one hand, researchers will, and do, have more contact with the worlds they aim to stimulate than ever before (not least through shared technology which, as I've mentioned, the original Bauhaus could never achieve), while on the other they have become much more thoughtful about the implications of what they are doing. Very, very different from the late 1970s where I began. I remember in the 1970s there was the story going the rounds about two designers sitting in the park: 'Let's be philosophical about this,' says one to the other, 'don't give it a second thought.' It was like that then. Well, today, students and researchers – forward-looking practitioners – seem to me to be deeply concerned with how to domesticate the new technologies; with the sustainability of materials; with design for an ageing population; with users; with 'think local, act global' and with design with *attitude*. Even with teams as well as individuals, as indeed they should be. If 'design for profit' was the catchphrase of the early 1980s – it was the title of a famous seminar at 10 Downing Street in 1984, hosted by Mrs Thatcher – the new catchphrase is 'design for people', which can, of course, be very profitable indeed. 'People' implying much more cultural diversity than there is today. How these two tendencies – new technology, plus a healthy suspicion of the implications of technology – manage to mesh with one another, is high on the agenda of young artists, craftspeople and designers today. The general idea is that the lion should lie down with the lamb, rather than on top of it. I certainly don't see the future as an educational global village where all the students sit in their huts, in a latter-day version of a Victorian tableau called 'And when did you last see your tutor?'

In addition to being *an agency of professional education* and *a research institute*, our new Bauhaus will be a place for learning *through* art and design as well as learning *to* art and design. What do I mean by this? Well, this is where the great poet and critic Herbert Read comes in handy. In 1944, he wrote an important book called *Education Through Art*. In it, he made the key distinction between what he called teaching *to* art, and what he called teaching *through* art. Teaching *to* art, he said, meant the professional education of the artist; teaching someone the skills and procedures and attitudes of how to become a practising artist. That aspect of art education, he said, seemed to be widely understood if not always that well done. Teaching *through* art, he added, meant teaching a series of related conceptual and physical skills through the medium of art: problem-solving, making things, resourcefulness, independence of mind, flexible thinking, a sense of direction, preparation for an unpredictable world of employment (and if he was right about the

1940s he would certainly be right about today), learning to see as well as to look, to pick up on what's in the ether, and so on. Herbert Read concluded that the very best form of art education should combine the two – teaching *to* art and teaching *through* art – but that teachers ought to be clear about which they were teaching at any given time. In Herbert Read's view – and this was very controversial – art and craft were the basis of every natural form of education, with all sorts of implications for social life and the conduct of everyday affairs. Of course, the dividing line between *to* and *through* is much less clear-cut today, as is the word 'art'. But the argument still holds.

Now, as you'll have gathered, this new Bauhaus is partly in place already, and some of it owes its origin to the original version: the seeds of a new two-way relationship with the creative industries; an increasing emphasis on action research as well as teaching; two-way relationships, long-established, with the professions of art, craft and design; and increasing success in graduate destinations, particularly over the last decade with the expansion of opportunities in the creative sector. All component elements of art-and-craft-education-as-crucible. It is one model of the way *all* education should be going. The seeds are there, but they need more fertile soil, more confidence and more respect. They need clearer thinking – and a vision, a Gropius-style manifesto, perhaps. There are so many misunderstandings outside the hermetic world of arts educators.

Finally, since the watchwords of the new creative industries are 'challenging the boundaries', 'multi-disciplinarity' and 'why not?', our new Bauhaus will be a place of *convergence*, challenging the old disciplinary boundaries between technologies and materials which go right back to Walter Crane's Arts and Crafts curriculum via the original Bauhaus.

Convergence at many different levels: between the present and the past, as history is reworked to supply a culture of quotations; between fine art and design – in the twentieth century, often at loggerheads – as both activities, with the applied arts or crafts in between, become part of a seamless spectrum as they are becoming in the professional world; between technology and design, as on the one hand engineers and industrial designers begin to work more closely together, and on the other, as digital and electronic technologies in studios and workshops mean that, for the first time in the long history of art and design education, the technology available to students is very similar to the technology they will be using in their professional lives; between making, prototyping and reproducing; between design and packaging, in the post-black-box era; between the applied arts and design, at the levels of batch-production and architectural detailing; and above all between the world inside the academy and the expanding world of the creative industries, both of them complementary parts of knowledge interchange – a convergence which implies a re-evaluation of that well-known pejorative 'the academy'. A convergence which brings with it a new role for the artist or craftsperson as well: as social commentator; as someone who puts a spanner in the works; as a maker in these new contexts.

In short, a convergence between the head, the heart and the hand.

*The head*: a more thoughtful, reflective attitude towards craft and design – research into craft, research through craft, craft as research. The workshop as laboratory. An explicit exploration of the links between the crafts and sustainability; small is beautiful; local and global; customisation; a critique of anonymous marketing; mass customisation; the importance of the distinctive kinds of knowledge and skills arising from the crafts.

*The hand*: the modern crafts, with their proliferation of subdivisions that would make even Polonius dizzy; including craftspeople, makers, artist-craftspeople, designer-craftspeople, designer-makers, applied artists, decorative artists, tragical-historical-pastoral and so on. These can now be seen as a range of possibilities rather than as inhibitors: the crafts as spectrum and the more inclusive and varied and versatile the better, as part of a culture of innovation. What distinguishes them, makes them highly visible is the care with which the things have been made, the fact that they have been made by one human being for another, the individual 'take', the use of materials and the thoughtfulness of their design. They can represent an ethical statement, but they needn't. In addition, there are the possibilities of batch production allied to customisation, and the crossovers between the crafts and digital technologies – a way of reuniting the crafts with manufacturing and with 'industries of one'. Plus the confident reintroduction of the crafts into the intellectual debates of the moment, around the creative industries.

*The heart*: which has nothing to do with sentiment, but rather with having one's finger on the pulse of what is going on in the broader visual culture and in the creative industries. We're told that our economy will, in the future, partly be driven by 'information' and 'intellectual property'. Well, our new Bauhaus will provide distinctive versions of both. Our students should read the *Economist* as well as the lifestyle magazines.

It was John Ruskin who originally said – in reaction against the old Gradgrindish 'cast-rated' system of art education which had been introduced into Victorian Britain and exported overseas – during a Manchester lecture given in 1859 and later published in *The Two Paths*, that the education of a young artist should always be a matter of the *head* and *heart* and *hand* going together. If the language seems old-fashioned, remember that out of the Arts and Crafts came the Bauhaus – and from there, much that has happened since within art education:

> ... Art must always be produced by the subtlest of all machines, which is the human hand. No machine yet contrived or hereafter contrivable, will ever equal the fine machinery of the human fingers. Thoroughly perfect art is that which proceeds from the heart,

which involves all the noble emotions, associates these
with the head, yet as inferior to the heart; and the
hand, yet as inferior to the heart and head; and thus
brings out *the whole man*.

The head, the heart and the hand. An 'association' which can
create the sort of knowledge modern society and the modern
economy so desperately need, and what's more so desperately
want. It is the role of the new Bauhaus to be a crucible for that
sort of knowledge, and to reflect on its implications. 'A genuinely contemporary expression of life', as Pevsner said of the
original Bauhaus – only this time round for real.